MW00975799

Apache Solr High Performance

Boost the performance of Solr instances and troubleshoot real-time problems

Surendra Mohan

BIRMINGHAM - MUMBAI

Apache Solr High Performance

First published: March 2014

Production Reference: 1180314

Published by Packt Publishing Ltd.
Livery Place
35 Livery Street
Birmingham B3 2PB, UK.

ISBN 978-1-78216-482-1

www.packtpub.com

Cover Image by Glain Clarrie (glen.m.carrie@gmail.com)

Credits

Author
Surendra Mohan

Reviewers
Azaz Desai
Ankit Jain
Mark Kerzner
Ruben Teijeiro

Acquisition Editor
Neha Nagwekar

Content Development Editor
Poonam Jain

Technical Editor
Krishnaveni Haridas

Copy Editors
Mradula Hegde
Alfida Paiva
Adithi Shetty

Project Coordinator
Puja Shukla

Proofreaders
Simran Bhogal
Ameesha Green
Maria Gould

Indexers
Monica Ajmera Mehta
Mariammal Chettiyar

Graphics
Abhinash Sahu

Production Coordinator
Saiprasad Kadam

Cover Work
Saiprasad Kadam

About the Author

Surendra Mohan, who has served a few top-notch software organizations in varied roles, is currently a freelance software consultant. He has been working on various cutting-edge technologies such as Drupal and Moodle for more than nine years. He also delivers technical talks at various community events such as Drupal meet-ups and Drupal camps. To know more about him, his write-ups, and technical blogs, and much more, log on to http://www.surendramohan.info/.

He has also authored the book *Administrating Solr*, *Packt Publishing*, and has reviewed other technical books such as *Drupal 7 Multi Sites Configuration* and *Drupal Search Engine Optimization*, *Packt Publishing*, and titles on Drupal commerce and ElasticSearch, Drupal-related video tutorials, a title on Opsview, and many more.

I would like to thank my family and friends who supported and encouraged me in completing this book on time with good quality.

About the Reviewers

Azaz Desai has more than three years of experience in Mule ESB, jBPM, and Liferay technology. He is responsible for implementing, deploying, integrating, and optimizing services and business processes using ESB and BPM tools. He was a lead writer of *Mule ESB Cookbook, Packt Publishing*, and also played a vital role as a trainer on ESB. He currently provides training on Mule ESB to global clients. He has done various integrations of Mule ESB with Liferay, Alfresco, jBPM, and Drools. He was part of a key project on Mule ESB integration as a messaging system. He has worked on various web services and standards and frameworks such as CXF, AXIS, SOAP, and REST.

Ankit Jain holds a bachelor's degree in Computer Science Engineering from RGPV University, Bhopal, India. He has three years of experience in designing and architecting solutions for the Big Data domain and has been involved with several complex engagements. His technical strengths include Hadoop, Storm, S4, HBase, Hive, Sqoop, Flume, ElasticSearch, Machine Learning, Kafka, Spring, Java, and J2EE.

He also shares his thoughts on his personal blog at `http://ankitasblogger.blogspot.in/`. You can follow him on Twitter at `@mynameisanky`. He spends most of his time reading books and playing with different technologies. When not at work, Ankit spends time with his family and friends, watching movies, and playing games.

> I would like to thank my parents and brother for always being there for me.

Mark Kerzner holds degrees in Law, Maths, and Computer Science. He has been designing software for many years and Hadoop-based systems since 2008. He is the President of SHMsoft, a provider of Hadoop applications for various verticals, and a cofounder of the Hadoop Illuminated training and consulting, as well as the coauthor of the *Hadoop Illuminated* open source book. He has authored and coauthored several books and patents.

> I would like to acknowledge the help of my colleagues, in particular Sujee Maniyam, and last but not least, my multitalented family.

Ruben Teijeiro is an experienced frontend and backend web developer who had worked with several PHP frameworks for over a decade. His expertise is focused now on Drupal, with which he had collaborated in the development of several projects for some important organizations such as UNICEF and Telefonica in Spain and Ericsson in Sweden.

As an active member of the Drupal community, you can find him contributing to Drupal core, helping and mentoring other contributors, and speaking at Drupal events around the world. He also loves to share all that he has learned by writing in his blog, `http://drewpull.com`.

> I would like to thank my parents for supporting me since I had my first computer when I was eight years old, and letting me dive into the computer world. I would also like to thank my fiancée, Ana, for her patience while I'm geeking around the world.

www.PacktPub.com

Support files, eBooks, discount offers and more

You might want to visit www.PacktPub.com for support files and downloads related to your book.

Did you know that Packt offers eBook versions of every book published, with PDF and ePub files available? You can upgrade to the eBook version at www.PacktPub.com and as a print book customer, you are entitled to a discount on the eBook copy. Get in touch with us at service@packtpub.com for more details.

At www.PacktPub.com, you can also read a collection of free technical articles, sign up for a range of free newsletters and receive exclusive discounts and offers on Packt books and eBooks.

http://PacktLib.PacktPub.com

Do you need instant solutions to your IT questions? PacktLib is Packt's online digital book library. Here, you can access, read and search across Packt's entire library of books.

Why Subscribe?

- Fully searchable across every book published by Packt
- Copy and paste, print and bookmark content
- On demand and accessible via web browser

Free Access for Packt account holders

If you have an account with Packt at www.PacktPub.com, you can use this to access PacktLib today and view nine entirely free books. Simply use your login credentials for immediate access.

Table of Contents

Preface

Solr is a popular and robust open source enterprise search platform from Apache Lucene. Solr is Java based and runs as a standalone search server within a servlet container such as Tomcat or Jetty. It is built in the Lucene Java search library as the core, which is primarily used for full-text indexing and searching. Additionally, the Solr core consists of REST-like HTML/XML and JSON APIs, which make it virtually compatible with any programming and/or scripting language. Solr is extremely scalable, and its external configuration allows you to use it efficiently without any Java coding. Moreover, due to its extensive plugin architecture, you can even customize it as and when required.

Solr's salient features include robust full-text search, faceted search, real-time indexing, clustering, document (Word, PDF, and so on) handling, and geospatial search. Reliability, scalability, and fault tolerance capabilities make Solr even more demanding to developers, especially to SEO and DevOp professionals.

Apache Solr High Performance is a practical guide that will help you explore and take full advantage of the robust nature of Apache Solr so as to achieve optimized Solr instances, especially in terms of performance.

You will learn everything you need to know in order to achieve a high performing Solr instance or a set of instances, as well as how to troubleshoot the common problems you are prone to facing while working with a single or multiple Solr servers.

What this book covers

Chapter 1, *Installing Solr*, is basically meant for professionals who are new to Apache Solr and covers the prerequisites and steps to install it.

Chapter 2, *Boost Your Search*, focuses on the ways to boost your search and covers topics such as scoring, the dismax query parser, and various function queries that help in boosting.

Chapter 3, Performance Optimization, primarily emphasizes the different ways to optimize your Solr performance and covers advanced topics such as Solr caching and SolrCloud (for multiserver or distributed search).

Chapter 4, Additional Performance Optimization Techniques, extends *Chapter 3, Performance Optimization*, and covers additional performance optimization techniques such as fetching similar documents to those returned in the search results, searching homophones, geospatial search, and how to avoid a list of words (usually offensive words) from getting searched.

Chapter 5, Troubleshooting, focuses on how to troubleshoot the common problems, covers methods to deal with corrupted and locked indexes, thereby reducing the number of files in the index, and how to truncate the index size. It also covers the techniques to tackle issues caused due to expensive garbage collections, out-of-memory, too many open files, and infinite loop exceptions while playing around with the shards. Finally, it covers how to update a single field in all the documents without completing a full indexation activity.

Chapter 6, Performance Optimization with ZooKeeper, is an introduction to ZooKeeper and its architecture. It also covers steps to set up, configure, and deploy ZooKeeper along with the applications that use ZooKeeper to perform various activities.

Appendix, Resources, lists down the important resource URLs that help aspirants explore further and understand the topics even better. There are also links to a few related books and video tutorials that are recommended by the author.

What you need for this book

In an intention to run most of the examples in the book, you will need a XAMPP or any other Linux-based web server, Apache Tomcat or Jetty, Java JDK (one of the latest versions), Apache Solr 4.x, and a Solr PHP client.

A couple of concepts covered in this book require additional software/tools such as the Tomcat add-on and ZooKeeper.

Who this book is for

Apache Solr High Performance is for developers or DevOps who have hands-on experience working with Apache Solr and who are targeting to optimize Solr's performance. A basic working knowledge of Apache Lucene is desirable so that the aspirants get the most of it.

Conventions

In this book, you will find a number of styles of text that distinguish between different kinds of information. Here are some examples of these styles, and an explanation of their meaning.

Code words in text, database table names, folder names, filenames, file extensions, pathnames, dummy URLs, user input, and Twitter handles are shown as follows: "Let us start by adding the following index structure to the fields section of our schema.xml file."

A block of code is set as follows:

```
<field name="wm_id" type="string" indexed="true" stored="true"
required="true" />
<field name="wm_name" type="text" indexed="true" stored="true"
termVectors="true" />
```

Any command-line input or output is written as follows:

```
# http://localhost:8983/solr/select?q=sonata+string&mm=2&qf=wm_name&defTy
pe=edismax&mlt=true&mlt.fl=wm_name&mlt.mintf=1&mlt.mindf=1
```

New terms and **important words** are shown in bold. Words that you see on the screen, in menus or dialog boxes for example, appear in the text like this: "Clicking on the **Next** button moves you to the next screen."

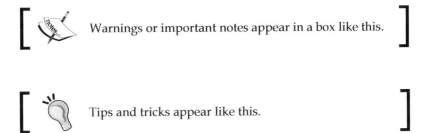

Warnings or important notes appear in a box like this.

Tips and tricks appear like this.

Reader feedback

Feedback from our readers is always welcome. Let us know what you think about this book—what you liked or may have disliked. Reader feedback is important for us to develop titles that you really get the most out of.

To send us general feedback, simply send an e-mail to feedback@packtpub.com, and mention the book title via the subject of your message.

If there is a topic that you have expertise in and you are interested in either writing or contributing to a book, see our author guide on www.packtpub.com/authors.

Customer support

Now that you are the proud owner of a Packt book, we have a number of things to help you to get the most from your purchase.

Downloading the example code

You can download the example code files for all Packt books you have purchased from your account at http://www.packtpub.com. If you purchased this book elsewhere, you can visit http://www.packtpub.com/support and register to have the files e-mailed directly to you.

Errata

Although we have taken every care to ensure the accuracy of our content, mistakes do happen. If you find a mistake in one of our books—maybe a mistake in the text or the code—we would be grateful if you would report this to us. By doing so, you can save other readers from frustration and help us improve subsequent versions of this book. If you find any errata, please report them by visiting http://www.packtpub.com/submit-errata, selecting your book, clicking on the **errata submission form** link, and entering the details of your errata. Once your errata are verified, your submission will be accepted and the errata will be uploaded on our website, or added to any list of existing errata, under the Errata section of that title. Any existing errata can be viewed by selecting your title from http://www.packtpub.com/support.

Piracy

Piracy of copyright material on the Internet is an ongoing problem across all media. At Packt, we take the protection of our copyright and licenses very seriously. If you come across any illegal copies of our works, in any form, on the Internet, please provide us with the location address or website name immediately so that we can pursue a remedy.

Please contact us at copyright@packtpub.com with a link to the suspected pirated material.

We appreciate your help in protecting our authors, and our ability to bring you valuable content.

Questions

You can contact us at questions@packtpub.com if you are having a problem with any aspect of the book, and we will do our best to address it.

1
Installing Solr

In this chapter, we will understand the prerequisites and learn how to install Apache Solr and the necessary components on our system. For the purpose of demonstration, we will be using Windows-based components. We will cover the following topics:

- Prerequisites for Solr
- Installing web servers
- Installing Apache Solr

Let's get started.

Prerequisites for Solr

Before we get ready for the installation, you need to learn about the components necessary to run Apache Solr successfully and download the following prerequisites:

- **XAMPP for Windows** (for example, V3.1.0 Beta 4): This can be downloaded from `http://www.apachefriends.org/en/xampp-windows.html`

  XAMPP comes with a package of components, which includes Apache (a web server), MySQL (a database server), PHP, PhpMyAdmin, FileZilla (an FTP server), Tomcat (a web server to run Solr), Strawberry Perl, and a XAMPP control panel

- **Tomcat add-on**: This can be downloaded from `http://tomcat.apache.org/download-60.cgi`

- **Java JDK**: This can be downloaded from `http://java.sun.com/javase/downloads/index.jsp`

- **Apache Solr**: This can be downloaded from `http://apache.tradebit.com/pub/lucene/solr/4.6.1/`

- **Solr PHP client**: This can be downloaded from `http://code.google.com/p/solr-php-client/`

 It is recommended that you choose the latest version of the preceding components due to the fact that the latest version has security patches implemented, which are lacking in the older ones. Additionally, you may use any version of these components, but keep in mind that they are compatible with each other and are secure enough to handle intruders.

Installing components

Once you have the previously mentioned installers ready, you may proceed with the installation by performing the following steps:

1. Install XAMPP and follow the instructions.

2. Install the latest Java JDK.

3. Install Tomcat and follow the instructions.

4. By now, there must be a folder called /xampp in your C: (by default). Navigate to the xampp folder, find the xampp-control application, and start it, as shown in the following screenshot:

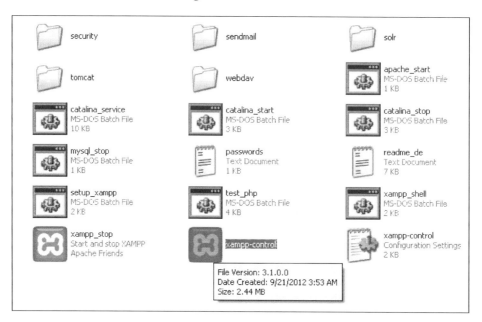

5. Start Apache, MySQL, and Tomcat services, and click on the **Services** button present at the right-hand side of the panel, as shown in the following screenshot:

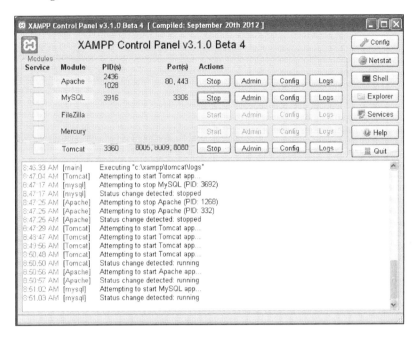

6. Locate **Apache Tomcat Service**, right-click on it, and navigate to **Properties**, as shown in the following screenshot:

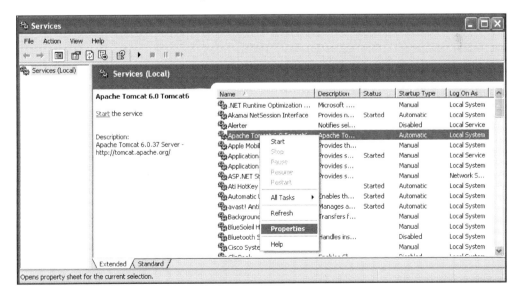

7. After the Properties window pops up, set the **Startup type** property to **Automatic**, and close the window by clicking on **OK**, as shown in the following screenshot:

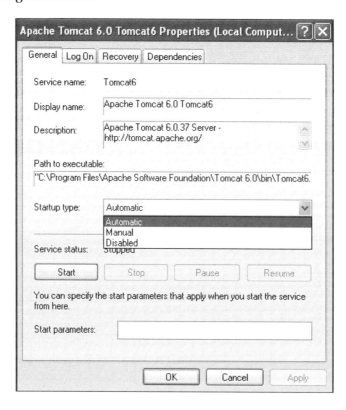

8. For the next few steps, we will stop Apache Tomcat in the **Services** window. If this doesn't work, click on the **Stop** option.

9. Extract Apache Solr and navigate to the /dist folder. You will find a file called solr-4.3.1.war, as shown in the following screenshot (we need to copy this file):

10. Navigate to `C:/xampp/tomcat/webapps/` and paste the `solr-4.3.1.war` file (which you copied in the previous step) into the `webapps` folder. Rename `solr-4.3.1.war` to `solr.war`, as shown in the following screenshot:

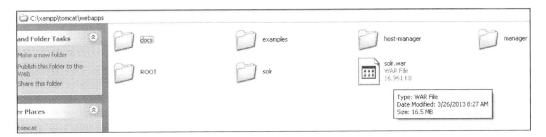

11. Navigate back to `<ApacheSolrFolder>/example/solr/` and copy the `bin` and `collection1` files, as shown in the following screenshot:

12. Create a directory in `C:/xampp/` called `/solr/` and paste the `ApacheSolrFolder>/example/solr/` files into this directory, that is, `C:/xampp/solr`, as shown in the following screenshot:

13. Now, navigate to C:/xampp/tomcat/bin/tomcat6, click on the **Java** tab, and copy the command -Dsolr.solr.home=C:\xampp\solr into the **Java Options** section, as shown in the following screenshot:

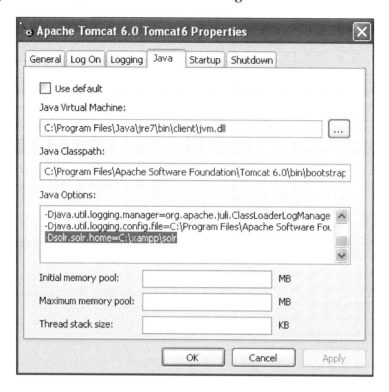

14. Now its time to navigate to the **Services** window. Start Apache Tomcat in the **Services** window.

15. Now, you are done with installing Apache Solr in your local environment. To confirm, type http://localhost:8080/solr/admin/ and hit the *Enter* key on the keyboard. You should be able to see Apache Solr's dashboard.

Summary

In this chapter, we have learned about the prerequisites necessary to run Apache Solr successfully and how to install and configure XAMPP, Tomcat, the Solr server, and the Solr client. In the next chapter, we will learn the different ways to boost our search using query parsers and various robust function queries such as field references, function references, and function query boosting based on different criteria.

2
Boost Your Search

In this chapter, we will learn different ways to boost our search using query parsers and various robust function queries such as field reference, function reference, and function query boosting based on different criteria. We will cover the following topics:

- Scoring
- The dismax query parser
- Function queries

So, let us get started.

Scoring

You might come across scenarios where your search engine should be capable enough to search and display appropriate search results from a large collection of documents, especially when the visitor is not really sure of what he/she intends to search.

In this section, we will learn about the basic concepts of how Solr ranks the documents and later step into how we can tweak the way Solr ranks and renders the search results.

We must keep in mind that the score is not a term that holds an absolute value; instead, it holds a relative value with respect to the maximum score and is normalized to fall between 0 and 1.0. The primary objective behind implementing a score is to narrow down the field list to a smaller set by mapping the fields together and then inject the smaller set to the search engine. Doing so helps the search engine understand the request better and serve the requester in a more appropriate way.

To understand the preceding objective better, let us assume we have an event that possesses more than 50 distinct fields. Of course, it would be quite confusing for the search engine to consider all the field values and render the search results, which results in an inappropriate result set. To simplify these fields, we map them into five categories or sections: who, what, where, how, and when. Now, we push the values of these five sections of the document to the search engine and the engine throws appropriate search results because all these fields are quite descriptive and are enough for the search engine to process.

Lucene follows a scoring algorithm, which is also known as the *tf.idf* model. There are a set of scoring factors that are associated with this model, which are as follows:

- **The term frequency (tf)**: This denotes the count when a term is found in a document's field, regardless of the number of times it appears in some other field. The greater the tf value, the higher the score.

- **The inverse document frequency (idf)**: Contrary to term frequency, in idf, the rarer the occurrence of a term, the higher is the score. To go deeper into idf, document frequency is the frequency of a document's occurrence on a per-field basis, and, as the name suggests, idf is the other way round.

- **The coordination factor (coord)**: It is the frequency of the occurrence of term queries that match a document; the greater the occurrence, the higher is the score. To be more specific, suppose that you have a document that matches a multiple term query (though, it doesn't match all the terms of that query). You may further reword documents that match even more terms using the co-ordination factor, which is directly proportional to the matched terms; that is, the greater the number of terms matched, the higher is its coordination factor.

- **The field length (fieldNorm)**: Considering the number of indexed terms, the shorter the matching field, the greater the document score. For instance, we have terms *Surendra* and *Surendra Mohan* (along with the other documents) in the index, and the user searches for the term `Surendra`. Under scoring, the field length would be higher in case of the former, that is, `Surendra`, than the latter due to the fact that it has one word, while the other has two.

The previously discussed factors are the vital components that contribute to the score of a document in the search results. However, these factors are not limited to that. You have the flexibility to introduce other components of the score as well, which is referred to as boosting. Boosting can be defined as a simple multiplier to a field's score, either in terms of an index or the query-time or any other parameter you can think of.

By now, you might be eager to explore further about such parameters and how they are formulated for use. For this, you may refer to `http://lucene.apache.org/core/4_0_0/core/org/apache/lucene/search/similarities/Similarity.html`, which will provide you with the additional information on their usage.

Query-time and index-time boosting

Before we actually get into the details of how to boost query-time and index-time, let us understand these terms for a better understanding of the actual concept.

- **Query-time**: It is the duration (in milliseconds) a query takes to run and process the search results. Let me remind you, this doesn't include the time taken to stream back the response.

- **Index-time**: It is the duration (in milliseconds) taken by the Solr instance to crawl the contents of the site and create their associated indices.

Index-time boosting

During index-time, you have the feasibility to boost a specific document either at the document level or at the field level. In document-level boosting, each field is boosted based on a value. Since it is rarely used and is highly uncommon due to the fact that it is not as flexible compared to query-time, we will discuss query-time in detail.

Query-time boosting

Think of a scenario wherein you would like a clause in your query string to contribute even further to the score. As you might be aware, a value less than 0 and 1 degrades the score, whereas a value greater than 1 enhances it. In the following example, we will learn how to boost the score by adding a multiplier.

Let us assume, we search for authors who either have the name Surendra or have a name that contains the word Mohan. The following is the query that suffices our requirement:

```
author_name: Surendra^3 OR Mohan
```

The preceding query will boost the search for the author name Surendra three times more than usual; however, it will render search results with author names that contain either Surendra or Mohan, considering results for Surendra as the prior ones.

Now, let us search for an author with the name Surendra, considering the names Mohan and Singh as optional, wherein we are not interested much about the search results rendered for the author name Singh. The following is the query:

```
+Surendra Mohan Singh^0.3
```

In the preceding query, we have mainly concentrated on the author name Surendra, considering the names Mohan and Singh as optional, and have degraded the score for the term Singh (as it wouldn't matter whether any record gets displayed in the search result for the term Singh or not).

We can also use the qf parameter of the dismax query parser to boost the score. This is because the qf parameter not only lists down the fields to search, but also facilitates a boost for them. In the *Dismax query parser* section of the chapter, we will cover how to use the dismax parser's qf parameter to boost.

Troubleshoot queries and scores

Consider a scenario wherein you have already boosted some keywords to appear at the top of the search results, and unfortunately, you can't find it at the top. Isn't it frustrating? Of course, it is quite frustrating, and we have a way to debug it so as to understand why the document is missing or is not at the expected position in the search results. You may enable the query debugging using the debugQuery query parameter.

Let us consider an example wherein we wanted the author with the name Surendra to get the top scores, but due to some reason, it didn't work out. Here is an example fuzzy query:

```
author_name: Surendra~
```

Now, let us execute the preceding query with debugQuery=on, and ensure that you are monitoring the original indentation by using the **View Source** feature of your browser. We assume that the top score is 3.657304, and there are two documents that match but none of them contains Surendra. One has Surena and the other has Urenda, as shown in the following code:

```
<doc>
<float name="score">3.657304</float>
<str name="author_name>Surena</str>
</doc>
<doc>
<float name="score">3.657304</float>
<str name="author_name">Urenda</str>
</doc>
```

```
<doc>
<float name="score">2.4632481</float>
<str name="author_name">Surendra Mohan</str>
</doc>
```

The first two documents (which are at the top of the search results) differ from Surendra just by two characters. The third document actually matched Surendra; however, it failed to overtake the top two due to a comparatively low score. You might think of banging your head! Don't worry, let us debug the issue and look into the debug output. We will skip the second document (that is, with the author name as Urenda) as it holds the same score as the first one. The debug output is as follows:

```
<lst name="explain">
<str name="Author:227132">
3.657304 = (MATCH) sum of:
3.657304 = (MATCH) weight(author_name:surena^0.42857146 in 286945),
product of:
0.20176922 = queryWeight(author_name:surena^0.42857146),
product of:
0.42857146 = boost
13.204025 = idf(docFreq=1, numDocs=399182)
0.035655525 = queryNorm
13.204025 = (MATCH) fieldWeight(author_name:surena in 286945),
product of:
1.0 = tf(termFreq(author_name:surena)=1)
13.204025 = idf(docFreq=1, numDocs=399182)
1.0 = fieldNorm(field=author_name, doc=286945)
</str>
<!-- skipping 2nd document ...-->
<str name="Author:93855">
2.4632481 = (MATCH) sum of:
2.4632481 = (MATCH) weight(author_name:surendra^0.75 in 9796),
product of:
0.32859424 = queryWeight(author_name:surendra^0.75),
product of:
0.75 = boost
12.287735 = idf(docFreq=4, numDocs=399182)
0.035655525 = queryNorm
7.6798344 = (MATCH) fieldWeight(author_name:surendra in 9796),
product of:
1.0 = tf(termFreq(author_name:surendra)=1)
12.287735 = idf(docFreq=4, numDocs=1002272)
0.625 = fieldNorm(field=author_name, doc=9796)
</str>
```

The preceding debug output is a mathematical breakdown of the different components of the score for us to analyze and debug the shortfalls. We can see that surena was allocated a query-time boost of 0.43, whereas it was 0.75 for surendra. We would have expected this due to the fact that fuzzy matching gives a higher weightage to stronger matches, and it happened here as well.

We shouldn't forget that there are other factors that are equally responsible for pulling the final score in a different direction. Let us now focus on the fieldNorm values for each one of them.

We can see that the fieldNorm value for the term surena is 1.0, whereas it is 0.625 for the term surendra. This is because the term we wanted to score higher had a field with more indexed terms (two indexed terms in case of Surendra Mohan), and just one for Surena on the other hand. Thus, we can say that Surena is a closer match than Surendra Mohan as far as our fuzzy query Surendra~ is concerned.

By now, we are in a better position as we figured out the reason behind this behavior. Now, it's time to find a solution that really works for us, though our expected search is not far behind the actual one. Firstly, let us lowercase our query, that is, author_name: surendra~ instead of author_name: Surendra~ to ensure that there isn't a case difference. If this solution doesn't work out, enable omitNorms in the schema. Even if this solution doesn't solve the purpose, you may try out other options, such as SweetSpotSimilarity. Please refer to http://lucene.apache.org/core/3_0_3/api/contrib-misc/org/apache/lucene/misc/SweetSpotSimilarity.html to explore further on this option.

The dismax query parser

Before we understand how to boost our search using the dismax query parser, we will learn what a dismax query parser is and the features that make it more demanding than the Lucene query parser.

While using the Lucene query parser, a very vital problem was noticed. It restricts the query to be well formed, with certain syntax rules that have balanced quotes and parenthesis. The Lucene query parser is not sophisticated enough to understand that the end users might be laymen. Thus, these users might type anything for a query as they are unaware of such restrictions and are prone to end up with either an error or unexpected search results.

To tackle such situations, the dismax query parser came into play. It has been named after Lucene's DisjunctionMaxQuery, which addresses the previously discussed issue along with incorporating a number of features that enhance search relevancy (that is, boosting or scoring).

Now, let us do a comparative study of the features provided by the dismax query parser with those provided by the Lucene query parser. Here we go:

- Search is relevant to multiple fields that have different boost scores
- The query syntax is limited to the essentiality
- Auto-boosting of phrases out of the search query
- Convenient query boosting parameters, usually used with the function queries (we will cover this in our next section, *Function queries*)
- You can specify a cut-off count of words to match the query

I believe you are aware of the q parameter, how the parser for user queries is set using the defType parameter, and the usage of qf, mm, and q.alt parameters. If not, I recommend that you refer to the Dismax query parser documentation at https:// cwiki.apache.org/confluence/display/solr/The+DisMax+Query+Parser.

Lucene DisjunctionMaxQuery

Lucene DisjunctionMaxQuery provides the capability to search across multiple fields with different boosts.

Let us consider the following example wherein the query string is mohan; we may configure dismax in such a way that it acts in a very similar way to DisjunctionMaxQuery. Our Boolean query looks as follows:

```
fieldX:mohan^2.1 OR fieldY:mohan^1.4 OR fieldZ:mohan^0.3
```

Due to the difference in the scoring of the preceding query, we may infer that the query is not quite equivalent to what the dismax query actually does. As far as the dismax query is concerned, in such scenarios, (in case of Boolean queries) the final score is taken as the sum for each of the clauses, whereas DisjunctionMaxQuery considers the highest score as the final one. To understand this practically, let us calculate and compare the final scores in each of the following two behaviors:

Fscore_dismax = 2.1 + 1.4 + 0.3 = 3.8

Fscore_disjunctionMaxQuery = 2.1 (the highest of the three)

Based on the preceding calculation, we can infer that the score produced out of the dismax query parser is always greater than that of the DisjunctionMaxQuery query parser; hence, there is better search relevancy provided that we are searching for the same keyword in multiple fields.

Now, we will look into another parameter, which is known as `tie`, that boosts the search relevance even further. The value of the `tie` parameter ranges from 0 to 1, 0 being the default value. Raising this value above 0 begins to favor the documents that match multiple search keywords over those that were boosted higher. Value of the `tie` parameter can go up to 1, which means that the score is very close to that of the Boolean query. Practically speaking, a smaller value such as 0.1 is the best as well as an effective choice we may have.

Autophrase boosting

Let us assume that a user searches for `Surendra Mohan`. Solr interprets this as two different search keywords, and depending on how the request handler has been configured, either both the terms or just one would be found in the document. There might be a case wherein one of the matching documents `Surendra` is the name of an organization and they have an employee named `Mohan`. It is quite obvious that Solr will find this document and it might probably be of interest to the user due to the fact that it contains both the terms the user typed. It is quite likely that the document field containing the keyword `Surendra Mohan` typed by the user represents a closer match to the document the user is actually looking for. However, in such scenarios, it is quite difficult to predict the relative score, though it contains the relevant documents the user was looking for.

To tackle such situations and improve scoring, you might be tempted to quote the user's query automatically; however, this would omit the documents that don't have adjacent words. In such a scenario, dismax can add a phrased form of the user's query onto the entered query as an optional clause. It rewrites the query as follows:

```
Surendra Mohan
```

This query can be rewritten as follows:

```
+(Surendra Mohan) "Surendra Mohan"
```

The rewritten query depicts that the entered query is mandatory by using + and shows that we have added an optional phrase. So, a document that contains the phrase `Surendra Mohan` not only matches that clause in the rewritten query, but also matches each of the terms individually (that is, `Surendra` and `Mohan`). Thus, in totality, we have three clauses that Solr would love to play around with.

Assume that there is another document where this phrase doesn't match, but it has both the terms available individually and scattered out in there. In this case, only two of the clauses would match. As par Lucene's scoring algorithm, the coordination factor for the first document (which matched the complete phrase) would be higher, assuming that all the other factors remain the same.

Configuring autophrase boosting

Let me inform you, autophrase boosting is not enabled by default. In order to avail this feature, you have to use the `pf` parameter (phrase fields), whose syntax is very much identical to that of the `qf` parameter. To play around with the `pf` value, it is recommended that you start with the same value as that of `qf` and then make the necessary adjustments.

There are a few reasons why we should vary the `pf` value instead of `qf`. They are as follows:

- The `pf` value helps us to use varied boost factors so that the impact caused due to phrase boosting isn't overwhelming.
- In order to omit fields that are always a single termed, for example, identifier, due to the fact that in such a case there is no point in searching for phrases.
- To omit some of the fields having numerous text count in order to retain the search performance to a major extent.
- Substitute a field with the other having the same data, but are analyzed differently. You may use different text analysis techniques to achieve this, for example, Shingle or Common-grams. To learn more about text analysis techniques and their usage, I would recommend you to refer to `http://wiki.apache.org/solr/AnalyzersTokenizersTokenFilters`.

Configuring the phrase slop

Before we learn how to configure the phrase *slop*, let us understand what it actually is. *Slop* stands for term proximity, and is primarily used to factorize the distance between two or more terms to a relevant calculation. As discussed earlier in this section, if the two terms `Surendra` and `Mohan` are adjacent to each other in a document, that document will have a better score for the search keyword `Surendra Mohan` compared to the document that contains the terms `Surendra` and `Mohan` spread individually throughout the document. On the other hand, when used in conjunction with the `OR` operator, the relevancy of documents returned in the search results are likely to be improved. The following example shows the syntax of using *slop*, which is a phrase (in double quotes) followed by a *tilde* (~) and a number:

```
"Surendra Mohan"~1
```

Dismax allows two parameters to be added so that *slop* can be automatically set; `qs` for any input phrase queries entered by the user and `ps` for phrase boosting. In case the *slop* is not specified, it means there is no *slop* and its value remains 0. The following is the sample configuration setting for *slop*:

```
<str name="qs" >1</str>
<str name="ps">0</str>
```

Boosting a partial phrase

You might come across a situation where you need to boost your search for consecutive word pairs or even triples out of a phrase query. To tackle such a situation, you need to use edismax, and this can be configured by setting pf2 and pf3 for word pairs and triples, respectively. The parameters pf2 and pf3 are defined in a manner identical to that of the pf parameter. For instance, consider the following query:

```
how who now cow
```

This query becomes:

```
+(how who now cow) "how who now cow" "how who" "who now" "now cow"
"how who now" "who now cow"
```

> This feature is unaffected by the ps parameter due to the fact that it is only applicable to the entire phrase boost and has no impact on partial phrase boosting.
>
> Moreover, you may expect better relevancy for longer queries; however, the longer the query, the slower its execution. To handle this situation and make the longer queries execute faster, you need to explore and use text analysis techniques such as Shingle or Common-grams.

Boost queries

Apart from the other boosting techniques we discussed earlier, boost queries are another technique that impact the score of the document to a major extent. Implementing boost queries involves specifying multiple additional queries using the bq parameter or a set of parameters of the dismax query parser. Just like the autophrase boost, this parameter(s) gets added to the user's query in a very similar fashion. Let us not forget that boosting only impacts the scores of the documents that already matched the user's query in the q parameter. So, to achieve a higher score for a document, we need to make sure the document matches a bq query.

To understand boost queries better and learn how to work with them, let us consider a realistic example of a music composition and a commerce product. We will primarily be concerned about the music type and the composer's fields with the field names wm_type and wm_composer, respectively. The wm_type field holds the Orchestral, Chamber, and Vocal values along with others and the wm_composer field holds the values Mohan, Webber, and so on.

We don't wish to arrange the search results based on these parameters, due to the fact that we are targeting to implement the natural scoring algorithm so that the user's query can be considered relevant; on the other hand, we want the score to be impacted based on these parameters. For instance, let us assume that the music type chamber is the most relevant one, whereas vocal is the least relevant. Moreover, we assume that the composer Mohan is more relevant than Webber or others. Now, let us see how we can express this using the following boost query, which would be defined in the request handler section:

```
<str name="bq">wm_type:Chamber^2 (*:* -wm_type:Vocal)^2 wm_
composer:Mohan^2</str>
```

Based on the search results for any keyword entered by the user (for instance, Opera Simmy), we can infer that our boost query did its job successfully by breaking a tie score, wherein the music type and composer names are the same with varied attributes.

In practical scenarios, to achieve a better and desired relevancy boost, boosting on each of the keywords (in our case, three keywords) can be tweaked by examining the debugQuery output minutely. In the preceding boost query, you must have noticed (*:* -wm_type:Vocal)^2, which actually boosts all the documents except the vocal music type. You might think of using wm_type:Vocal^0.5 instead, but let us understand that it would still add value to the score; hence, it wouldn't be able to serve our purpose. We have used *:* to instruct the parser that we would like to match all the documents. In case you don't want any document to match (that is, to achieve 0 results), simply use -*:* instead.

Compared to function queries (covered in the next section), boost queries are not much effective, primarily due to the fact that edismax supports multiplied boost, which is obviously demanding compared to addition. You might think of a painful situation wherein you want an equivalent boost for both the Chamber wm_type and Mohan wm_composer types. To tackle such situations, you need to execute the query with debugQuery enabled so as to analyze the scores of each of the terms (which is going to be different). Then, you need to use disproportionate boosts so that when multiplied by their score (resultant scores from debugQuery) ends up with the same value.

Boost functions

Boost functions provide a robust way to add or multiply the results of a user-specific formula (this refers to a collection of function queries that is covered in the next section of this chapter, *Function queries*) to a document's score. In order to add to the score, you can specify the function query with the `bf` parameter. As mentioned earlier, dismax adds support for multiplying the results to the score, and this can be achieved by specifying the function query with the boost parameter. The best part of using `bf` and `boost` parameters is that there is no limitation in terms of the number of times you can use them.

Let us now understand how to use boost functions by taking forward our music composition and the commerce product example. We would like to boost the composition tracks by how frequently they were viewed (that is, how popular the track is among users):

```
<str name="boost">recip(map(rord(wm_track_view_cou
nt),0,0,99000),1,95000,95000)</str>
```

Note that we don't have any space within the function. The `bf` and `boost` parameters are parsed in a different manner. You may have multiple boost functions within a single `bf` parameter, each separated by space. This is an alternative to using multiple `bf` parameters. You may also implement a multiplied boost factor to the function with bf by appending `^150` (or another value) at the end of the function query. It is equivalent to using the `mul()` function query.

Boost addition and multiplication

If you have overcome the difficulty in additive boosting (the `bf` parameter), you would probably be satisfied enough with the scoring. However, let me tell you that multiplicative boosting (the `boost` parameter) is even easier to use, especially in situations where the intended boost query is less than or equal to the user query (normally true).

Let us assume a scenario where you want a score of 75 percent of the document to come from the user query and the remaining 25 percent from our custom formula (or any defined ratio). In such cases, I would recommend that you use additive scores. The trick behind choosing an appropriate boost is that you should be aware of the top score required for the best match on the user query with an intention to manipulate the proportions appropriately. Just as an exercise, try an exact match on the title, which is normally the highest boost field in a query and record the top score rendered. Repeat this process a number of times on varied documents. For instance, the highest score achieved in your user query lands to `1.2`, and you intend the function query to boost up half as much as the user query does on the final score.

Simply adjust the function query so that its upper limit is set to `0.6` (which is half of the highest score) and multiply with this(assuming you already have the function query that lies in the 0–1 range). Even if the preceding guidelines don't work out for you, you need to tune these additive scores. This is actually tricky due to the fact that Lucene responds to each and every change you do, especially by modifying the `queryNorm` part of the score in the background which you can't control. During the process, it is recommended to keep an eye on the overall ratio, which is a desirable value between the user query and the boost, and not on a specific score value. This attempt of playing around with the queries to achieve the highest score of a user query might lead to a problem such as a change in the highest score of the user query due to the change in data. It is highly recommended to keep this process in continuous monitoring to avoid any such problems from occurring. If you want to explore further and learn more about how to monitor these background activities, please refer to *Chapter 2, Monitoring Solr* of *Administrating Solr, Packt Publishing*.

The other angle of your thought on using the `boost` function is a multiplier to the user query score (factor). The best part of using a factor is that you don't need to worry what the best user query score is; it's got nothing to do with in this context. Since multiplicative boost has a relative impact on what you are looking for, the tricky part of it is weighing your boost (that is, considering the weightage of the boost). If your function query lies in the 0–1 range, it achieves the same weight as that of the user query. When you increase your function's values above 0, this means you are trying to reduce the influence relative to the user query. For instance, if you add `0.6` to your 0–1 range such that the upper end of the range shifts from 1 to 1.6, it is weighed approximately half of what you added. The following formula is considered:

Result: (1.6-1)/2 = 0.3

Function queries

A function query can be defined as a user-specified Solr function that is usually mathematical in nature and is supported by dismax, edismax, and other standard query parsers. It enables you to generate a relevancy score based on the actual value of one or more numeric fields. Since function queries are technical, they are so robust that they can be used in instances where the queries' context comes into picture. The instances include searching, filtering, faceting, sorting, and so on.

Now, we will understand a few of the ways by which we can incorporate a function query into our Solr instance. They are as follows:

- **The dismax query parser** (the `bf` and `boost` parameters): As we already discussed earlier in this chapter, the `bf` and `boost` parameters boost the user query score by adding or multiplying the function query. In the upcoming section, we will learn how to derive a function query in depth using a few examples.

- **The boost query parser**: Unlike the `boost` parameter in dismax, the boost query parser gives you an option to specify a function query that is multiplied to the user query. On the other hand, the query is parsed by the Lucene query parser, which is not the case with dismax. Here is a sample query:

  ```
  {!boost b=log(wm_type)} wm_composer:Mohan
  ```

- **The lucene query parser** (the `_val_` pseudo field): The following is a sample query:

  ```
  wm_composer:Mohan && _val_:"log(wm_type)"^0.02
  ```

  In the preceding query, don't get an impression that `_val_` is a field; instead, it triggers the query parser to treat the quoted portion of it as a function query rather than a field value. Since this query matches all the documents, it is suggested to combine it with other necessary clauses to ensure more accurate results.

- **The function query parser** (`func`): The `func` function query parser is primarily used in debugging a function query. You may also do some calculations while querying, which would look something as follows:

  ```
  q= {!func}add($val1,$val2)$val1=max(price, 200)$val2=2.0.
  ```

- The following is an example URL snippet:

  ```
  q=log(wm_composer) &defType=func&fl=wm_composer,score
  ```

- The score of each document in the result set is the outcome of the function query.

- **The function range query parser** (`frange`): The `frange` query parser is similar to the `func` query parser with an additional capability to filter out the documents in the search results whose resulting scores fall in a specific range (which can be defined). It takes two parameters, `l` and `u`, which denote the lower and upper ends of the range, respectively. It also takes two more parameters that are Boolean in nature and are called `incl` and `incu` to specify whether the lower and/or upper ends are inclusive. For your information, they are inclusive by default and can be altered as and when required. The following is a sample URL snippet:

  ```
  q={!frange l=0 u=2.5}sum(wm_user_ranking,wm_composer_ranking)
  ```

- **Sorting**: Along with sorting capabilities on field values, Solr facilitates sorting on function queries as well. The following is an example URL snippet wherein we sort results by distance:

```
q=*:*&sort=dist(2, p1, p2) asc
```

Field references

To use fields in a function query, we need to keep the following constraints in mind (identical to those of sorting):

- Firstly, the field must be indexed and not multivalued.

- Secondly, while using text fields, you need to make sure they are analyzed down to one token.

- Additionally, just like sorting, all the field values are stored in the field cache. This means that you need to make sure there is enough memory available to store the field cache items, along with having an appropriate query stated in newSearcher of solrconfig.xml so as to avoid the first search being hit with the initialization cost.

- In case the field value for a document is unavailable, the result will definitely be 0 and numeric values for the corresponding numeric field. But did you think what would be the scenario in case of other field types? In case of TrieDateField, you get the ms() value. If the value is 0, can you imagine how ambiguous this would be because 0 as the date value might mean 2000 or blank! For historical date fields, we get the ord() value. It is unexpected, but it is a fact that true is denoted by 2 and false by 1 in case of Boolean fields. You also get the ord() value for text fields which is the same as that of the historical date fields. You might come across situations wherein you need to make some functions work with text values. In such a scenario, you need to explicitly use the literal() function. You might be wondering looking at ms() and ord(). Don't worry! We will cover them in depth in our upcoming section.

Function references

In this section, we will cover a reference to most of the function queries in Solr.

You may have an argument to a function as a constant, probably a numeric value, a field reference, or a function embedded into it. You can do an interesting thing by fetching any argument into a new request parameter in the URL (you are free to name the request parameter whatever you like) and reference it with $ prefixed to it, which will be something as follows:

```
&defType=func&q=max(wm_composer,$min) &min=30
```

You have the flexibility to either have the parameter in the request or have it configured to the request handler configuration.

Mathematical operations

Basic mathematical operations and constants are covered in the following listed functions:

- `sum(a, b, c, …)`: This function is an alias of `add()` and it adds all the arguments stated in `(a, b, c, ….. )`
- `sub(a, b)`: This function subtracts `b` from `a` and is equivalent to the expression `a-b`
- `product(a, b, c, …)`: This function is an alias of `mul()` and multiplies the arguments together
- `div(a, b)`: This function divides `a` by `b` and is equivalent to the expression `a/b`
- `log(a)`: This function gives the base 10 logarithm value of `a`
- `ln(a)`: This function gives the natural logarithm value

To learn more about the other mathematical functions such as `sqrt(a)`, `cbrt(a)`, `ceil(a)`, `floor(a)`, `rint(a)`, `pow(a,b)`, `exp(a)`, and `e()`, I would recommend that you visit the `java.lang.Math` API at `http://docs.oracle.com/javase/6/docs/api/java/lang/Math.html`.

The following are a few of the geometric and/or trigonometric functions that we commonly use:

- `rad(a)`: This function converts degrees to radians
- `deg(a)`: This function converts radians to degrees
- `sin(a)`, `cos(a)`, `tan(a)`, `asin(a)`, `acos(a)`, `atan(a)`, `sinh(a)`, `cosh(a)`, `tanh(a)`, `hypot(a,b)`, `atan2(b,a)`, `pi()`: I recommend that you refer to the `java.lang.Math` API for the explanation of these functions
- **Geospatial functions**: I would recommend that you refer to the GeoSpatial search section of *Chapter 1, Searching Data* of *Administrating Solr, Packt Publishing*

We will now look into a few more mathematical functions that are very useful and equally straightforward to use. They are as follows:

- `map (a, min, max, output, ops?)`: If a lies between `min` and `max` (inclusive of the `min` and `max` values), then `output` is returned. In case `ops` (the optional parameter) is passed, it is returned when a doesn't lie between `min` and `max` inclusive; else, a itself is returned. It is more useful when you deal with the default values or wish to bind a between some threshold values (`min` and `max`).

- `max (x, y)`: This function returns the value greater than x and y.

- `scale (a, minTarget, maxTarget)`: This function returns a such that it is scaled to be between `minTarget` and `maxTarget`. For instance, if the value of a is found exactly at the center of the largest and smallest values of a across all documents, a is returned as half of the distance between `minTarget` and `maxTarget`.

- `linear(a,b,c)`: It is a macro for `sum(product(b,a), c)`.

- `recip (a,b,x,c)`: It is a macro for `div(x, linear(a,b,c))`.

The ord() and rord() functions

As mentioned earlier in the *Field reference* section of this chapter, `ord(fieldRef)` implies for references to the text fields of a function query. The following is an overview of `ord()` and `rord()`:

- `ord(fieldRef)`: Assuming that we have an ascending sorted array for all unique indexed values for `fieldRef` (reference to a field), `ord(fieldRef)` returns the array position, that is, it returns the ordinal of a document's indexed value. The values are in the ascending order, 1 being the first position. In the case of position, the value returned is 0; this means that the array doesn't exist.

- `rord(fieldRef)`: This is the same as the value of `ord()`, with the difference being that it acts in reverse order.

Let us now understand `ord()` or `rord()` using a scenario. Assuming there are four documents that have been indexed with the holding values 60, 60, 85, and 90, respectively, for a field, say field x. In this situation, `ord(x)` is going to return values ranging from 1 to 3, even though we have four documents in the index. The reason behind this is that out of four documents, only three of them are distinct (fields where the value 60 has been repeated). There is another difference but a tricky one, that is, the original values are not in a linear pattern. They are more clustered together towards the higher values. In such cases, `ord()` and `rord()` linearize the data and end up with a loss of the distribution of the original value.

Other functions

In this section, we will learn different ways to use the `ms()` function (mentioned earlier in the *Field references* section of this chapter) to fetch a date/time value. Please note that its arguments are optional in nature. Also, any field reference to a time will act ambiguously to a blank value, ending up with a zero value. The following is the description of the `ms()` function:

- `ms(end_date?, start_date?)`: As stated earlier in this section, these arguments are optional in nature. So, if you don't provide any argument, it will return the current time. If you provide one argument (say, `ms(end_date)`), it will return the argument passed (in our case, it will return the value for `end_date`). If you pass both the arguments (say, `ms(end_date, start_date)`), the second argument (`start_date`) will be subtracted by the first one (`end_date`) and the difference in the two values will be returned; that is, the function returns a value for `end_date - start_date`.

There are a couple of function queries that return the score values of some other query. It is quite a niche feature that possesses its own usage, one of them being sorted based on whether the field has a value. The following are these function queries:

- `query (q, def?)`: This returns the document's score based on the query supplied as the first parameter. In case it doesn't match, a second parameter (optional) is returned if it is supplied; else it returns 0. During function query parsing, due to the query's uncooperative location, it can't be entered normally, or to be more specific, painlessly. You may put the query in another parameter and reference it, which will look something like this:

  ```
  query ($para) &para=wm_music_attrib:3
  ```

  Another thing you can do is specify it using `local-params` that has the query in `v`, which will look something like this:

  ```
  query ({!v="wm_music_attrib:3"}).
  ```

- `boost (q, boost)`: This is the same as the query (`q`) with the top up as the score being multiplied with the boost value (which is a constant).

  The following is another function query that calculates the distance between two strings based on a specified algorithm and the value ranges from 0 to 1:

- `strdist(s1, s2, alg)`: The first two arguments (`s1` and `s2`) denote the strings between which the distance needs to be computed. The `alg` argument denotes the algorithm to be used, which might be replaced by `jw` (Jaro Winkler), `ngram`, or `edit` (Levenshtein).

  There are a couple of ways to compute the geospatial distance, one of them being `geodist()`, which is described as follows:

- `geodist(...)`: It returns the geospatial distance between a pair of points on Earth using the Haversine formula. Each point is considered based on the first occurrence of an argument, the `pt` parameter, or the `sfield` parameter, out of which, at least two of them shouldn't be left blank. You may specify the point as an argument with either a field based on `LatLonType` or a pair of field names/constants, which are the typically used argument sorts to represent the latitude and the longitude. The following is an example for your reference:

```
geodist (store, 39.6, -67.8)
```

There is a pool of other function queries that haven't been covered here. I would recommend you refer to `http://wiki.apache.org/solr/FunctionQuery` to explore more on what more is in store and how they work.

If you want to dive deeper into the Haversine formula, I recommend you refer to `http://bigdatanerd.wordpress.com/2011/11/03/java-implementation-of-haversine-formula-for-distance-calculation-between-two-points/`.

Boosting the function query

The overall process that needs to be carried out in an intention to boost a function query is as follows:

- Select a formula whose plotted shape is desirable to you
- Input values specific to your data
- Decide and add the weight of the boost relative to the user query (say, for example, 25 percent or a quarter)
- Decide on either of the boosts (additive or multiplicative) and apply the relative weight based on the chosen approach (refer to the *Boost addition and multiplication* section)

To understand this better, we will go through a few examples that address common scenarios using in-built formulas.

If you wish to work on your custom formulas instead of using the in-built ones, I recommend you use tools such as the graphing calculator or Grapher (this comes with Mac OS X). You might urge yourself to use a spreadsheet, for instance, MS Excel, but this is not the appropriate tool for this purpose.

Moreover, in scenarios where your data keeps changing, with an impact of manual modification of the constants in the function query, I would recommend you implement a scheduled automated test on your Solr data to ensure that the Solr data fits in the expected bounds. To achieve this, you can probably configure a **Continuous Integration** (**CI**) server.

Logarithm

The logarithm formula is especially meant for inputs that grow without any bounds and also result in an unbounded output. However, it fails while handling larger values or numbers due to the fact that the growth of the curve gets hampered while addressing large numbers. The use of a logarithm is appropriate and ideal when you are looking for an output you might conclude with. It is highly recommended that you avoid negative scores in your logarithm, which means that it can't be inverted.

The following is the formula for an example graph:

logc((c-1)mx+1)

Here, *c* is a number of your choice, which is greater than 1, and is responsible for how the curve should bend, *m* is *(c-1)/horizon* (described next), and *x* is a non-negative input, which is usually a field reference. The graph of the preceding formula is as follows:

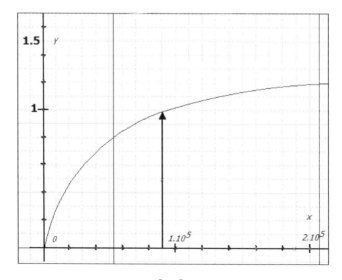

The recommended value for *c* is 10 (demonstrated in our preceding graph). The smaller the value of c, the more linear the output; on the other hand, the higher its value, the more the curve you get as the output will lean. *horizon* is considered as the inverse of *m* and its value results to 1. Using the logarithm, values advance the output gradually, but in a shallow slope that slowly gets even shallower. Assuming *c* as 10, here is a simplified Solr function query that is to be used:

```
log(linear(x,m,1))
```

If you intend to verify your formula, input the value as 0 that should result in 0, and then supply *horizon*, which should result in 1. If successful, you are now ready to proceed further by boosting your other function queries.

Reciprocal

Reciprocal is the formula that is more effective when you intend to achieve a maximum boost on an input 0 and descends as the input value increases. It is generally used to boost the newly added content based on the document's age.

The following is a sample graph that demonstrates the curve for the following formula:

c/(x+c)

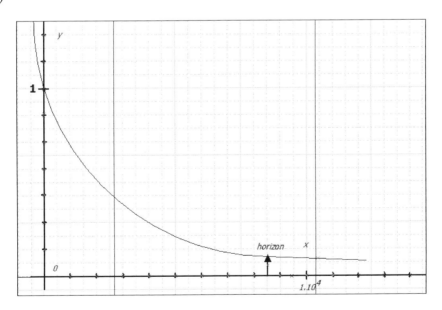

This is translated very easily to a Solr function query, which is `recip(x,1,c,c)`.

Here, x is a non-negative input, either a field or a function reference to a field, and c is one-tenth of the horizon input value (approximately). Thus, the larger the c value, the lesser is the boost effect.

Now, it's time to verify your formula. Input a value as 0, which should result in 1, and then supply *horizon*, which should result in a number ~0.09. If successful, you are now ready to proceed with further boosting on your other function queries.

Linear

The linear formula is favorable and recommended in situations wherein you are sure that the value you have in your schema or computed formula stays within a fixed range or is bound. Then, it becomes easy to shift this to a nominal range of 0–1 quite easily, assuming that the relationship between the input and the expected boost effect is linear in nature.

The formula is *linear (x,m,c)*.

Here, *x* is the input field, *m* is calculated as 1/(maxR-minR), c is calculated as minR/(minR-maxR), where maxR signifies the value of the range that has the maximum boost, and minR denotes the end of the range that has the least boost.

Suppose that you have the input value ranging from 4 to 10, and if 4 is least relevant compared to 10, minR is 4 and maxR is the other value, that is, 10.

To verify your formula, input values, each for minR and maxR, and record whether the output it is 0 or 1. An output as 1 denotes a higher boost. You are now ready to proceed with further boosting on your other function queries.

Inverse reciprocal

Generally speaking, the reciprocal of a linear function is favorable due to the fact that despite of the input growing without bounds, it results in a bounded output.

This is the sample graph that shows the curve for the following formula:

{(-max2 + max) / (mx + max-1)} + max

Here, *x* is a non-negative input, usually a field reference. *m* is *1/horizon* and *max* is the value that this function targets but doesn't reach (*1 < max < 2*, typically, *1.5*).

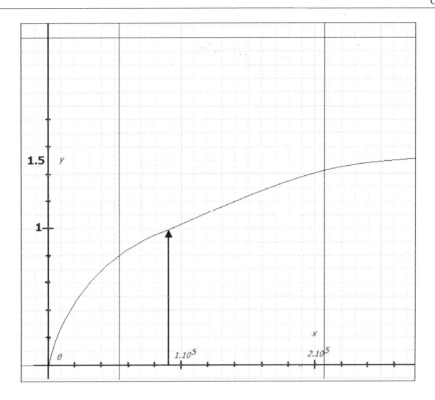

Use the following Solr function query:

```
sum (recip(x,m,a,c),max)
```

Here, x, m, and max are the same as described previously; a is max(1-max) and c is max-1.

If you intend to verify your formula, input a 0 value that should result in 0 and then supply *horizon*, which should result in 1. You are now ready to proceed with further boosting on your other function queries based on the formula you have in place.

Summary

In this chapter, we covered advanced topics associated with scoring, function queries, and so on. We began with a background on Lucene scoring, different terminologies and their significance, and learned query-time and index-time boosting. We also learned how to troubleshoot your queries and scoring and headed towards more complex and important topics such as different ways to use the dismax query parser and how it is better than Lucene's DisjunctionMaxQuery. Apart from this, we learned the ways of boosting our search based on varied circumstances, for instance, automatic phrase boosting and partial phrase boosting, what are the boost queries and boost functions and how can they be used. We also covered advanced concepts of function queries such as field and function references, different mathematical operations, including geometric or trigonometric operations, and how to implement formulas such as logarithm, reciprocal, and linear in an intention to boost your function queries.

In the next chapter, we will mainly concentrate on different techniques to optimize the Solr performance, which includes (but not limited to) various performance factors, how to replicate an index using the master-slave architecture, Solr caching, SolrCloud, how to scale your Solr playground horizontally (also known as how to play around with multiple Solr servers and sharding), and learn how to implement a real-time based search.

3
Performance Optimization

In this chapter, we will learn more different ways to optimize your Solr's performance, starting from understanding the required factors that affect performance and heading towards advanced concepts such as index replication using the master-slave architecture. We will also learn more about playing around with multiple Solr servers, sharding, distributed search, and much more. We will cover the following topics:

- Solr performance factors
- Solr caching
- Using SolrCloud
- Near real-time search

So, let us get started.

Solr performance factors

In this section, we will understand the factors and metrics that impact Solr's performance. The following are the metrics and the parameters that you should look into in order to see the impact of the changes you have performed:

- **Transactions Per Second (TPS)**: This denotes the number of search queries and document updates you are able to perform in a second. To have a better understanding, you may navigate to the statistics page and look at the `avgTimePerRequest` and `avgRequestsPerSecond` parameters of your request handler.

- **Memory usage**: While tweaking components to manage the memory usage, you need to ensure that the memory used by Solr doesn't increase day-by-day, though a slight increase in this may be acceptable. However, if this usage keeps increasing without any constraint, you will be prone to receive out-of-memory errors. In such a situation, TPS increases significantly, and extra care needs to be taken so as to debug and stabilize memory usage. You need to keep an eagle's eye on this memory-usage trend; to monitor this, you may use JConsole.

- **CPU usage**: It is also recommended that you keep an eye on Solr's CPU usage, probably using JConsole. There are OS-specific tools as well, such as PrefMon and Top, which have been designed for OS Windows and UNIX respectively, to monitor Solr-specific Java processes. Using these tools is helpful if you wish to monitor processes, in case it has a number of services running on the same box, fighting for the resources.

Solr caching

In this section, we will learn about the different caching techniques and ways to configure them appropriately so as to achieve better performance of your Solr instance.

Document caching

Document cache, one of the cache types available with us, stores Lucene's internal documents fetched from the disk. In order to get the document caching to work at its optimal level, you need to configure it appropriately so as to minimize I/O calls that result in boosted deployment performance.

Let us assume that we are dealing with the deployment of Solr, where we have approximately 100,000 documents to address. Additionally, our single Solr instance gets a maximum of 10 concurrent queries and each query can fetch 220 documents, which is the maximum count.

Based on the preceding parameters, our documentcache tag should look similar to the following code snippet (add the following code to your solrconfig.xml file):

```
<documentCache
  class="solr.LRUCache"
  size="2200"
  initialSize="2200"/>
```

Note that we didn't use the `autowarmCount` parameter. This is because the document cache makes use of Lucene's internal ID in order to identify documents, and these identifiers can't be copied during index changes. Hence, this cache can't be automatically warmed.

We will now understand the preceding code snippet and the impact of each parameter. Firstly, we defined it in the `documentCache` tag of our `solrconfig.xml` configuration file and specified a couple of parameters that define and impact the document cache's behavior. The `class` parameter instructs Solr about the Java class to be used during implementation. In our case, we have used `solr.LRUCache` as we have an intention to add more information into the cache than fetching from it. If you are fetching more information than you have added, it is recommended that you use the `size` parameter of `solr.FastLRUCache` instead of `solr.LRUCache`, which denotes the upper end size of the cache. It is always recommended to set the value of `size` as the product of the maximum number of results returned by a query and the number of concurrent queries. This ensures that we have enough cache space available and Solr doesn't need to fetch data from the index. The last parameter, which is `initialSize`, denotes the initial size of the cache. We have set the `initialSize` value to the same as that of the `size` value. This is because we don't have Solr to invest its resources for a cache resizing activity.

Once you have set the parameters, you need to keep monitoring its behavior; if you find your cache not meeting your expectations, you should take appropriate actions accordingly. While you make the changes, you should keep in mind that having a large cache with a very low hit rate can prove to be even worse than having no cache at all.

 While monitoring the cache usage, if you find expulsion, this is a signal that the cache might be too small. Additionally, if you get a very poor hit rate, it is usually recommended that you turn off the cache. As you already know, cache setup is dependent upon data, queries, and users; thus, it is highly recommended that you keep an eagle's eye on your cache and feel free to change them as and when required.

Query result caching

In the case of an enterprise web application or an e-commerce portal, multiple user queries are fired and handled when a user attempts to search for some specific information. We don't have any idea how many queries fired are unique in nature, and of course, it is not suggested to even predict that. If we can figure out the unique query count fired in a day, week, month, quarter, and year or during any specific duration, we can optimally use a query result cache. Yes, of course, by looking into Solr logs, you will be able to fetch the desired statistics to play around with.

Let us think of a scenario where you own an e-commerce web portal and your Solr instance handles 15 to 20 queries per second. Each query can be sorted based on three different fields (chosen by the user). Additionally, a user can also choose the sort order. Upon analyzing the logs for the previous quarter, we found that there are approximately three thousand unique queries that users have typed in the search box.

Based on the preceding statistics, it's now time to configure our query result cache, which is as follows. It should be added to our `solrconfig.xml` file:

```
<queryResultCache
  class="solr.LRUCache"
  size="18000"
  initialSize="18000"
  autowarmCount="4500"/>
```

The parameters such as `class`, `size`, and `initialSize` denote the same as we discussed in the *Document caching* section of this chapter.

However, it is good to understand the equation responsible for having the `size` parameter as `18000`. The lowest value that the `size` parameter can hold is as follows:

```
size = 3000 * 3 * 2
```

The formula for calculating the `size` parameter is as follows:

Size = (x * y) * 2

Here, *x* is the total number of unique queries fired by the users in the recorded duration and *y* = field count per user query.

Thus, `size = 18000` (in our case).

Additionally, we have set the `initialSize` parameter to the maximum size of `18000` so as to avoid wastage of resources while resizing the cache.

We will now understand the `autowarmCount` parameter, which we didn't cover earlier in this chapter. This parameter denotes the number of entries that should be copied when Solr invalidates the caches, for instance, after a commit operation has been performed. In our case, we have set this parameter as one fourth of the maximum size of the cache (*18000 / 4*), which is `4500`. This is because we don't want the caches to keep warming for a longer duration. Moreover, you are open to adjusting its value as and when required so as to achieve optimal Solr performance.

Like document caching, you need to keep an eye on how the cache is being used while your Solr instance performs its activities. If you find expulsion, there are chances that your cache is too small. If you analyze a very poor hit rate, it is wise to disable or turn off the query result caching. If the caching doesn't seem to perform its job as per your expectations, you may adjust the parameters as and when required.

Filter caching

In general scenarios, Solr developers are inclined to add an additional clause with a suitable logical operator to the main query, forgetting that Solr also provides filters to tackle such situations and is highly robust if it is used in a wise manner. These filter queries are capable enough to handle the scenarios that are practically solved by adding clauses through logical operators (which adds complexity to the queries). While using filter queries, an added advantage is that we can cache the filter results so as to minimize the resource usage overheads, resulting in better performance; the filter cache is the one for you to do the same.

Let us assume that in our same e-commerce web application (as discussed in the *Document caching* section), which is a single Solr slave instance handling all the queries coming out of the application. We also analyzed the log records for the previous quarter and found that we have approximately 3000 unique filter queries fired during this time span. We will now set up a filter cache based on the current statistics we have in hand. Add the following code snippet to your solrconfig.xml configuration file:

```
<filterCache
  class="solr.FastLRUCache"
  size="3000"
  initialSize="3000"
  autowarmCount="750"/>
```

First of all, let me remind you, parameters such as class, size, initialSize, and autowarmCount signify the same as we discussed earlier in the *Document caching* and *Query result caching* sections.

Here, as the class parameter, we have used solr.FastLRUCache instead of solr. LRUCache, because as per our investigation, we get more information that we added. Instead, you may use solr.LRUCache if it is the other way round, that is, you add more information than you fetch.

For the initialSize parameter, we have set the same value as that of size, as we want to avoid the overhead of cache resizing.

In the case of the last parameter, which is `autowarmCount`, we have again set this as one fourth of the maximum cache size because we don't want the cache to be warmed for a longer duration.

Like document and query result caching, you need to keep an eye on how the cache is being used while your Solr instance performs its activities. If you find expulsion, there are chances that your cache is too small. If you analyze a very poor hit rate, it is wise to disable or turn off the query result caching.

Result pages caching

Imagine a situation where you have an e-commerce online library and you know that your data hardly changes. You might be wondering how to make your search server a stress-free one! You might think of setting up caching, probably HTTP caching, which is of course a good idea. At this point, you will have an unanswered question on your mind, wondering whether you have to set up an external cache prior to Solr or whether you can instruct Solr to use its own cache mechanism that probably serves your purpose? The answer is yes, Solr has such mechanisms that can cache all the result pages, and we will learn how to implement them in this section.

We assume that you have basic knowledge of HTTP cache headers. If not, there is nothing to worry about; you may refer to the RFC document at `http://www.w3.org/Protocols/rfc2616/rfc2616-sec13.html` before you proceed further with this section.

Now it's time to configure the HTTP cache. We assume that our index changes every two hours. Let us perform the following steps, starting from configuring our Solr request dispatcher:

1. Replace the request dispatcher definition in `solrconfig.xml` with the following content:

```
<requestDispatcher handleSelect="true">
  <httpCaching lastModifiedFrom="openTime" etagSeed="Solr">
    <cacheControl>max-age=7200, public</cacheControl>
  </httpCaching>
</requestDispatcher>
```

2. Send a query very similar to the following ones so as to look into the HTTP headers:

```
http://localhost:8080/solr/select?q=author
```

3. Here we go with the HTTP headers:

```
HTTP/1.1 200 OK
Cache-Control: max-age=7200, public
Expires: Fri, 27 Dec 2013 18:45:55 GMT
Last-Modified: Fri, 27 Dec 2013 16:45:23 GMT
ETag: "XzEwNDEwNDEwNDEwNDEwNFOvbHC="
Content-Type: application/xml; charset=UTF-8
Transfer-Encoding: chunked
```

If you get a response as shown in the preceding code, this indicates that your cache configuration worked.

Now, let us go through the parameters and their respective values and understand them better. We have defined a cache inside the `requestDispatcher` tag. The `handleSelect="true"` attribute states that error handling is enabled (by default, it is set to `false`). Within the `httpCaching` tag, which is responsible for the configuration of HTTP caching in Solr, you must have noticed that the `<httpCaching never304="true" >` tag has been disabled as we are using `lastModifiedFrom="openTime"` and `etagSeed="Solr"` instead of `httpCachingnever304` (either `httpCachingnever304` or `lastModifiedFrom` and `etagSeed` can work together). This means that when you use `httpCachingnever304="true"`, the other two parameters are ignored.

The `lastModifiedFrom="openTime"` parameter denotes the last modified HTTP header that will be relative to the timestamp in which the current searcher was opened, which is relative to the previous replication execution timestamp. If you wish to make it relative to the timestamp when the physical index was last modified, you may use `dirLastMod` instead of `openTime`. Next, the `etagSeed` attribute is responsible for generating *ETag HTTP cache header*.

The `cacheControl` tag is used to specify the generation of the cache control HTTP headers. For instance, in our case, we have used `max-age=7200`, which denotes the maximum life span of the cache (2 hours) and instructs Solr to set the cache as invalid once this maximum life span has been elapsed. The public directive instructs Solr that the response is open to be cached by any cache type.

Using SolrCloud

As you might be aware, a new feature named SolrCloud was introduced in Apache Solr 4.0, and it enables us to perform searching and distributed indexing at a full scale. Prior to SolrCloud, the sharding concept was heavily used as far as managing a Solr distributed cluster was concerned. However, managing it was a challenge, which allowed the SolrCloud concept to come into play and made the activity even easier and more robust. Let us go through the challenges faced using sharding, the cons of which made SolrCloud exhale. They are as follows:

- **Maintenance of the index view**: Sharding restricts updations and deletions to be forwarded to the appropriate shard, to ensure there is only one version of each document.

- **Auto-failure recovery**: If a shard goes down, that portion of the index goes offline and you need to bring it up and run it manually with a backup.

- **Cluster configuration**: Using sharding in a distributed environment and managing schema.xml and solrconfig.xml can be quite painful and would require additional skills in terms of configuration deployment utilities to handle files in a cluster.

- **Durability**: Think of a situation where a document that has been indexed to a shard never writes to the disk when the shard goes down. Custom solutions need to be implemented to enforce durability.

- **Querying a cluster**: In case a shard goes down, this is an overhead to notify each and every application that queries Solr so that the shard lists can be changed. SolrCloud handles the preceding activities very efficiently, adding value to it with the following top-up list of incorporated features:

    ◦ **Built-in partitioning**: You just need to define a number of shards for the cluster, and it is left to Solr to manage the shard's partitioning schema. It is guaranteed that updation and deletion activities are sent to the correct shard.

    ◦ **Transaction log**: A transaction log is written to the disk, thereby providing durability.

    ◦ **Centralized configuration**: Cluster configuration is managed by ZooKeeper, which enables you to point to a configuration when you wish to start a shard in the cluster.

    ◦ **Auto-failover and replication**: This supports shard replication and auto-failover for the nodes of a cluster.

Let us now discuss in detail the various activities we can do using SolrCloud.

Creating a SolrCloud cluster

Imagine a situation where you find that the amount of data is too high to be handled by a single Solr server, and you need to set up a distributed environment. Yes, of course, you can set up another server or go for another master database that holds a unique set of data. While creating a SolrCloud cluster, you need to set up replication, address duplicate data, and other activities. We will discuss these activities in this section.

Before you go deeper into how to create a SolrCloud cluster, it is recommended that you understand how to set up, configure, and deploy ZooKeeper, all of which was covered in *Chapter 6, Performance Optimization with ZooKeeper* of this book.

Let us assume that we would like to create a SolrCloud cluster that has four Solr servers, and our data gets distributed among the Solr servers in such a way that we have the original data sharded in two machines. Additionally, we would like to have a copy of each shard available with us, which will act as a disaster recovery data in case any of our Solr instances go down. We also assume that we have our ZooKeeper cluster up and running at `192.168.1.4` (IP address) using the port 2181. Let us get started with the following steps:

1. Populate the cluster configuration into the ZooKeeper cluster. To do so, run the following command:

   ```
   java -Dbootstrap_confdir=./solr/collection1/conf -Dcollection.
   configName=twoShardsTwoReplicasConf -DnumShards=2
   -DzkHost=192.168.1.4:2181 -jar start.jar
   ```

2. Once our configuration has been populated, start another node (the shard) by running the following command:

   ```
   java -DzkHost=192.168.1.4:2181 -jar start.jar
   ```

3. By now, we have two shards created and we will replicate these shards. We simply need two additional servers for running the following command in order to get each replica (in our case, run the command twice):

   ```
   java -DzkHost=192.168.1.4:2181 -jar start.jar
   ```

We are now done with creating a SolrCloud cluster consisting of two nodes (shards) and their respective replicas. Wasn't it simple! To cross-check whether you have actually succeeded in creating the SolrCloud cluster, navigate to the cloud configuration of your Solr administration panel and you will find that your cluster has four nodes, the first two of them acting as leaders for the shards and the other two as their replicas. Now, you are in a position to get-set-go to start indexing data on one of the servers. From there, it's Solr's responsibility to handle data distribution and autoreplication of the corresponding data. Let us now understand what we did and why.

Firstly, we sent all our configuration files to ZooKeeper so that our Solr servers are capable enough to fetch it from there. That's the reason we added the `Dboostrap_confdir` and `-Dcollection.configName` parameters at the initial stage, that is, while running our first server. The first parameter signifies the directory location where we want our configuration files to be placed in ZooKeeper, and the second parameter contains the nomenclature of your configuration. The `-DnumShards=2` parameter states the number of shards we want to have in our cluster (in our case, it's 2). The `-DzkHost` parameter instructs Solr where to look for our ZooKeeper cluster (the IP address along with the port).

 While setting up the SolrCloud cluster, you need to be sure about the number of shards you want due to the fact that you can't modify the count once the cluster has been created. However, you can add replicas even after the cluster has been created, without touching the existing shard count.

It is feasible for you to run the ZooKeeper server while it is being embedded into your Solr instance. Let us learn how to do this.

To start your ZooKeeper server while it is being embedded into Solr, you need to pass the `-DzkRun` parameter instead of `-DzkHost=192.168.1.4:2181`. So, our command would look as follows:

```
java -Dbootstrap_confdir=./solr/collection1/conf -Dcollection.configName=
twoShardsTwoReplicasConf -DnumShards=2 -DzkRun -jar start.jar
```

Multiple collections within a cluster

Think of a situation where we want more than one collection within a single Solr cluster. For instance, we want to store books in one collection and authors in the other. Let us learn how to do it using SolrCloud.

Before we go deeper into the actual concept that we intend to cover, we again recommend that you understand how to set up, configure, and deploy ZooKeeper. This is covered in *Chapter 6, Performance Optimization with ZooKeeper* of this book. We assume that our ZooKeeper is running on the localhost and is listening on port 2181. Let us now get started with the following steps:

1. Since we don't have any collections defined so far in our new SolrCloud cluster that we wish to start, we have to start with the `solr.xml` file. Your `solr.xml` file on both the instances should look like the following code snippet:

   ```
   <?xml version="1.0" encoding="UTF-8"?>
   <solr persistent="true">
   ```

```
<cores adminPath="/admin/cores"
   defaultCoreName="collection1" host="${host:}"
   hostPort="${jetty.port:}"
   hostContext="${hostContext:}"
   zkClientTimeout="${zkClientTimeout:15000}">
</cores>
</solr>
```

2. Next, let us assume that our SolrCloud cluster constitutes of two SolrCloud instances, both running on the same physical server on ports 8983 and 9999 respectively. Start these two instances using the following commands:

    ```
    java -Djetty.port=8983 -DzkHost=localhost:2181 -jar start.jar
    ```

    ```
    java -Djetty.port=9999 -DzkHost=localhost:2181 -jar start.jar
    ```

3. Now, it's time to add the configuration files for both the collections to ZooKeeper. Let us assume that we want the configuration files to be stored for both collections at /usr/share/config/books/conf and /usr/share/config/authors/conf respectively. In order to send these files to their respective locations in ZooKeeper, let us run the following commands from our $SOLR_HOME directory:

    ```
    cloud-scripts/zkcli.sh -cmdupconfig -zkhost localhost:2181
    -confdir /usr/share/config/books/conf -confnamebookscollection
    ```

    ```
    cloud-scripts/zkcli.sh -cmdupconfig -zkhost
    localhost:2181 -confdir /usr/share/config/authors/conf
    -confnameauthorscollection
    ```

4. By now, we have the configuration files pushed to ZooKeeper and they are now in place. It's time to create our collections for books and authors. To do so, run the following commands:

    ```
    curl 'http://localhost:8983/solr/admin/collections?action=CREATE&n
    ame=bookscollection&numShards=2&
    replicationFactor=0'
    curl 'http://localhost:8983/solr/admin/collections?action=CREATE&n
    ame=authorscollection&numShards=2&replicationFactor=0'
    ```

5. Finally, we are done with our procedure and it's time to test whether everything went well. Let us query one of the newly created collections. Here we go:

    ```
    curl
    'http://localhost:8983/solr/authorscollection/select?q=*:*'
    ```

6. The response to the preceding command is as follows:

```xml
<?xml version="1.0" encoding="UTF-8"?>
<response>
  <lst name="responseHeader">
    <int name="status">0</int>
    <int name="QTime">39</int>
    <lst name="params">
    <str name="q">*:*</str>
  </lst>
  </lst>
    <result name="response" numFound="0" start="0" maxScore="0.0">
  </result>
</response>
```

As you can see, the response works correctly; however, you might have noticed that we get 0 documents due to the fact that we don't have any data indexed. Additionally, while querying the other collection, that is, books, you can expect the same response.

Let us now walk through what we did and what exactly happened. As you might have noticed, we used the same solr.xml file on both the instances and none of them contained any information associated to the core. We have done this purposely as we want a clean and tidy cluster without any collection created. Please keep in mind, before the configuration files are sent to ZooKeeper, our configuration directories should consist of solrconfig.xml, schema.xml, and stopwords.txt so as to facilitate our Solr instance work.

Now, let us understand the zkcli.sh script, which is an interesting and important script that we used to push the configuration files to ZooKeeper. This can be found in the cloud-scripts directory of our Solr distribution. The cmd parameter specifies that we intend to do. In our case, we used upconfig, which states that we wish to upload the configuration files. The zkhost parameter defines the IP address and the port of our ZooKeeper instance. The confdir parameter is one of the most important and crucial parameters and specifies the path to the directory (in our case, /usr/share/config/books/conf and /usr/share/config/authors/conf) holding the Solr configuration files. The last parameter, confname, states the name of the collection we are going to use along with our configuration.

Once the configuration files are pushed into ZooKeeper, we run the command to create the actual collection in the cluster. To do this, we send a request to the /admin/collections handler, which is based on the collections API. We instruct Solr to create a new collection using the action=CREATE parameter and collection name by using name=bookscollection and name=authorscollection. The last two parameters we use are numShards and replicationFactor, which signify the number of shards and replicas respectively that we intend to have.

Managing a SolrCloud cluster

On the top of creating new collections using the API facilitated by SolrCloud, we can also attempt additional operations with the intention to manage our SolrCloud cluster dynamically. They are the delete and reload operations, where the delete operation helps you delete your existing collection and the reload operation helps you reload the whole collection. Let us learn them in this section.

We assume that you have already referred to the preceding section, *Multiple collections within a cluster*. We will continue with the previous example where we created two collections with the names bookscollection and authorscollection.

1. Let us delete one of the collections, for instance, authorscollection. To do so, run the following command:

    ```
    curl 'http://localhost:8983/solr/admin/collections?action=DELETE&n
    ame=authorscollection'
    ```

2. To verify whether the preceding command did its job, you may navigate to the cloud section of your Solr administration panel. In our case, we found that the collection authorscollection was missing, that is, it was deleted successfully.

3. Now, let us understand how collection reload works. Prior to the actual activity, we will update the spellings.txt file that is found in the conf directory in /usr/share/config/books/. The original file consists of the following text:

    ```
    pizza
    history
    ```

4. Once the spellings.txt file is updated, it should contain the following text:

    ```
    fiction
    comedy
    ```

5. In order to reload the collection, we need to update the collection configuration in ZooKeeper and later carry on with the actual reload command. So, to update the collection configuration in ZooKeeper, we will run the following command from our Solr home directory:

```
cloud-scripts/zkcli.sh -cmdupconfig -zkhost localhost:2181
-confdir /usr/share/config/books/conf –confnamebookscollection
```

6. By now, we have the latest version of the configuration files associated with `bookscollection` in ZooKeeper. To perform the actual reload activity, we will run the following command:

```
curl 'http://localhost:8983/solr/admin/collections?action=RELOAD&n
ame=bookscollection'
```

7. To ensure that our preceding activities impacted ZooKeeper positively, we will run the following command:

```
curl 'http://localhost:8983/solr/bookscollection/admin/
file?file=spellings.txt'
```

8. We come up with a response that looks as follows:

```
fiction
comedy
```

By looking at the preceding response, we ensured that our reload activity worked appropriately.

Let us understand how it worked. We initiated our activity on a cluster that contained two collections (`authorscollection` and `bookscollection`). Our intention was to delete one of the collections (`authorscollection`) and update and reload the other one (`bookscollection`). To do so, we used Solr's collections API.

In order to delete the collection, we triggered the delete action (`action=DELETE`) on the collections API address (that is, `/solr/admin/collections`), and used the `name` parameter to specify the name of the collection we intend to delete. Once the command did its job, we cross-checked it in Solr's administration panel and found that the `authorscollection` collection was missing; hence, it was proved that the intended collection had been deleted successfully.

Later, we proceeded to update the other collection (`bookscollection`). In order to see how it works, we modified the content of the `spellings.txt` file and uploaded it to ZooKeeper by running the script, `zkcli.sh` (one of the scripts shipped with Solr). Then, we instructed Solr to reload our targeted collection by triggering the reload action (`action=RELOAD`) to the collection API along with the `name` parameter, which specifies the collection name we targeted to reload.

After the reload activity, we even cross-checked the effect by running a command that reads the content of `spellings.txt` using the `/admin/file` handler. To do so, we passed the `file=spellings.txt` parameter to this handler, which ensures that the content returned is the updated one.

Distributed indexing and searching

Imagine a situation where you have a distributed SolrCloud cluster, that is, you have a number of shards and their respective replicas. In such a scenario, the data will be automatically distributed among all the shards, will get replicated between the replicas, and will be spread throughout the shards. Additionally, you would definitely want them to be capable enough to be queried when a user attempts to search for a keyword or a set of keywords. It looks a bit tough to handle, but let me inform you that Solr 4.0 and higher versions can do this job without much complexity involved compared to the Solr versions below 4.0, where in the latter case, you have to manually specify the list of shards to be queried. In this section, we will learn how to execute queries, which are distributed in nature.

We assume that by now, you are familiar with how to create a SolrCloud cluster. In case you are not familiar with this, I recommend that you refer to the *Creating a SolrCloud cluster* section of this chapter.

Before we start with the actual steps to follow, let us assume that we have a SolrCloud cluster consisting of three nodes and a single cluster deployed to this cluster; it is the same as that of one collection with three shards. For demonstration purposes, we will use the example configuration files and the XML files as documents that are shipped with Solr and are placed in the `exampledocs` directory.

As far as distributed indexing and searching activity is concerned, the best part of working on Solr Version 4.0 and higher versions is that you simply need to send the appropriate index and search requests to one of the shards (no need to send to all the shards individually). To index the document files (that is, all XML files) of the `exampledocs` directory, we run the following command from the `exampledocs` directory of our Solr instance that is running on port 8983:

```
java -jar post.jar *.xml
```

To make sure the documents have been really sent to all the shards, we will use both non-distributed as well as distributed queries. Starting with the non-distributed queries, we will run three queries individually for each shard and record the respective response we get. We will do this by performing the following steps:

1. Run the following query for the first shard:

   ```
   curl 'http://localhost:8983/solr/select?q=*:*&rows=0&distrib=false'
   ```

2. We get the following response:

   ```
   <?xml version="1.0" encoding="UTF-8"?>
     <response>
       <lst name="responseHeader">
         <int name="status">0</int>
   ```

```
    <int name="QTime">0</int>
    <lst name="params">
      <str name="distrib">false</str>
      <str name="q">*:*</str>
      <str name="rows">0</str>
    </lst>
  </lst>
  <result name="response" numFound="3" start="0">
  </result>
</response>
```

3. Now, we run the following query for the second shard:

   ```
   curl 'http://localhost:5983/solr/select?q=*:*&rows=0&distrib=false'
   ```

4. We get the following response for the preceding query:

   ```
   <?xml version="1.0" encoding="UTF-8"?>
   <response>
    <lst name="responseHeader">
      <int name="status">0</int>
      <int name="QTime">0</int>
      <lst name="params">
          <str name="distrib">false</str>
          <str name="q">*:*</str>
          <str name="rows">0</str>
      </lst>
    </lst>
    <result name="response" numFound="7" start="0">
    </result>
   </response>
   ```

5. Next, we run the following query to our last, that is, the third shard:

   ```
   curl 'http://localhost:3983/solr/select?q=*:*&rows=0&distrib=false'
   ```

6. We get the following response for the preceding query:

   ```
   <?xml version="1.0" encoding="UTF-8"?>
   <response>
     <lst name="responseHeader">
     <int name="status">0</int>
     <int name="QTime">0</int>
     <lst name="params">
       <str name="distrib">false</str>
       <str name="q">*:*</str>
       <str name="rows">0</str>
     </lst>
   ```

```
    </lst>
    <result name="response" numFound="4" start="0">
    </result>
</response>
```

You might have noticed that the total number of documents returned as a result of the preceding three queries is 14. So far, everything seems to work perfectly.

7. Now, let us run the following distributed query (provided by Solr) to check whether all three shards have been queried or not:

```
curl 'http://localhost:8983/solr/select?q=*:*&fl=id,[shard]&rows=70'
```

8. We get the following response for the same (as the response was huge, I have considered one document per shard):

```
<?xml version="1.0" encoding="UTF-8"?>
  <response>
    <lst name="responseHeader">
      <int name="status">0</int>
      <int name="QTime">66</int>
      <lst name="params">
        <str name="fl">id,[shard]</str>
        <str name="q">*:*</str>
        <str name="rows">70</str>
      </lst>
    </lst>
    <result name="response" numFound="14" start="0"
maxScore="1.0">
    <doc>
      <str name="id">SM6371N</str>
      <str name="[shard]">gr0-vaio:3983/solr/collection1/ </str>
    </doc>
...............
  <doc>
    <str name="id">MS15020P</str>
    <str name="[shard]">gr0-vaio:5983/solr/collection1/ </str>
  </doc>
...............
  <doc>
    <str name="id">AI-01</str>
    <str name="[shard]">gr0-vaio:8983/solr/collection1/ </str>
  </doc>
...............
    </result>
  </response>
```

On looking at the response, we are assured that our distributed query worked as we intended to, by fetching the documents from all the three shards.

Let us now understand how it worked. We indexed the documents to the Solr instance running on port 8983. However, when we queried the shards individually with the distrib=false parameter, we noticed that each of the shards holds a different number of documents, which is totally expected. By now, you must have understood that the distrib=false parameter forced the query to run on the Solr server it was sent to and behave in a non-distributed manner.

Let us concentrate on the distributed query we had run. The q=*:* parameter was used to fetch all the documents and returned a maximum of 70 documents (row=70). Additionally, we specified the fl parameter in such a way that we instructed Solr to return the document with the id field and information about the shard from which the document was fetched (fl=id, [shard]). As you must have noticed, we received the response that fetched documents from all the shards associated with that collection. This is because when using SolrCloud deployment, Solr automatically queried all the shards in the cluster that were associated with a specific collection. As information about the shards and replicas (if any) are fetched from ZooKeeper anyway, we don't need to bother about passing such information explicitly in the query.

Stopping automatic document distribution

Imagine a situation where you want your users to search for the document they have indexed. In such a scenario, the standard distribution among SolrCloud instances cannot be a good solution; instead, you would like your document distribution to be controlled within the application (that is, outside Solr). Possibly, you might think of storing the documents on a per-user-per-shard basis. This means that you need to turn off automatic document distribution. We will learn how to do it in this section by performing the following steps:

1. We assume that you know how to create a SolrCloud cluster and play around with the fl parameter to modify the returned document.

2. Additionally, we assume that you have the following index structure defined in the schema.xml configuration file, and ZooKeeper already holds this file, which is up to date:

```
<fields>
    <field name="id" type="string" indexed="true" stored="true"
required="true" />
    <field name="usrName" type="string" indexed="true"
stored="true" />
    <field name="record" type="text" indexed="true" stored="true" />
```

```
    <field name="_version_" type="long" indexed="true"
stored="true"/>
</fields>
```

3. We consider two files `recordUserA.xml` and `recordUserB.xml`, each holding user data of users `userA` and `userB`, respectively. These files are as follows:

    ○   The `recordUserA.xml` file is as follows:

    ```
    <add>
        <doc>
            <field name="id">1</field>
            <field name="usrName">userA</field>
            <field name="record">userA record</field>
        </doc>
    </add>
    ```

    ○   The `recordUserB.xml` file is as follows:

    ```
    <add>
        <doc>
            <field name="id">2</field>
            <field name="usrName">userB</field>
            <field name="record">userB record</field>
        </doc>
        <doc>
            <field name="id">3</field>
            <field name="usrName">userB</field>
            <field name="record">Another record of userB</field>
        </doc>
    </add>
    ```

4. Now it's time to stop automatic distribution of documents among shards. In order to do so, we need to define the `UpdateRequestProcessorChain` tag in the `solrconfig.xml` file as follows:

```
<updateRequestProcessorChain>
    <processor class="solr.LogUpdateProcessorFactory" />
    <processor class="solr.RunUpdateProcessorFactory" />
    <processor class="solr.NoOpDistributingUpdateProcessorFactory" />
</updateRequestProcessorChain>
```

We also assume that you already have a cluster constituting at least two nodes that are up and running, and have a collection with the name `collection1` in place. Just so you know, we have one of our nodes running on the IP address `192.168.0.100` and the second one running on the IP address `192.168.0.101`; both on the same port, that is, `8983`.

5. We intend to manually distribute data to the respective Solr instances. In our example, we want the data of recordUserA.xml to be indexed to the Solr instance running at 192.168.0.100 and the data of recordUserB.xml to the one running at 192.168.0.101. So, we will index the data using the following commands:

```
java -Durl=http://192.168.0.100:8983/solr/collection1/update -jar
post.jar recordUserA.xml

java -Durl=http://192.168.0.101:8983/solr/collection1/update -jar
post.jar recordUserB.xml
```

6. By now, we have indexed the respective data to their corresponding Solr instances (as per our knowledge). However, it is better to test this by running the following Solr query, which distinguishes the indexed documents based on the shards on which they are stored:

```
curl http://localhost:5983/solr/select?q=*:*&fl=*,[shard]
```

7. The following is the response of the preceding command:

```
<?xml version="1.0" encoding="UTF-8"?>
<response>
  <lst name="responseHeader">
    <int name="status">0</int>
    <int name="QTime">20</int>
    <lst name="params">
      <str name="q">*:*</str>
      <str name="fl">*,[shard]</str>
    </lst>
  </lst>
  <result name="response" numFound="3" start="0" maxScore="1.0">
<doc>
  <str name="id">2</str>
  <str name="usrName">userB</str>
  <str name="record">userB record</str>
  <str name="[shard]"> 192.168.0.101:8983/solr/collection1/ </str>
</doc>
<doc>
  <str name="id">3</str>
  <str name="usrName">userB</str>
  <str name="record">Another record of userB</str>
  <str name="[shard]"> 192.168.0.101:8983/solr/collection1/ </str>
</doc>
<doc>
  <str name="id">1</str>
  <str name="usrName">userA</str>
```

```
    <str name="record">userA record</str>
    <str name="[shard]"> 192.168.0.100:8983/solr/collection1/ </str>
</doc>
</result>
</response>
```

Manually validating the preceding response, we can conclude that we have achieved what we intended to. So now, let us proceed further to understand what we did.

We defined the index structure consisting of three fields in the `schema.xml` file where the `_version_` field is internally used by Solr. Since our `schema.xml` file is quite simple to understand, let us skip it and proceed to the next one.

Let us look into a very interesting part of our activity, that is, the `UpdateRequestProcessorChain` tag's definition. Apart from the standard `solr.LogUpdateProcessorFactory` and `solr.RunUpdateProcessorFactory` processors, we have used `solr.NoOpDistributingUpdateProcessorFactory`, which restricts Solr from distributing the documents automatically; instead, it forces the update command to be indexed on the specific node it has been sent to.

We have used the `post.jar` library in order to index the data, and the `-Durl` parameter to specify on which server the data needs to be indexed. We used two servers (which were up and running) with their IP addresses as `192.168.0.100` and `192.168.0.101` to index data associated with the users `userA` and `userB` respectively. Once the indexing process was complete, we cross-checked it by running a query that returns all documents (`q=*:*`).

Additionally, we specified the `fl` parameter so that the response that was returned also contains the corresponding shards from where the documents were fetched along with the other three field values (`fl=*,[shard]`).

If you analyze the response, you will find that the data that belongs to `userA` has been fetched from the server running at `192.168.0.100` (`<str name="[shard]"> 192.168.0.100:8983/solr/collection1/ </str>`), and the remaining data that belongs to `userB` has been fetched from the other server running at `192.168.0.101` (`<str name="[shard]"> 192.168.0.101:8983/solr/collection1/ </str>`).

Once you turn off the automatic document distribution among the shards, you need to remember that the shards might be created unevenly. This is because the data is being pushed manually and the shard size will completely depend on the number of documents you push to each shard. Thus, it is recommended that you intelligently plan this manual distribution before you actually implement it.

Near real-time search

Before we learn about **near real-time search** (**NRT**), let us first understand what real-time search is. It is the ability to search for the appropriate content immediately after the content has been added or modified. This means that if you add or modify content, the system should be capable enough to process the content at such a high speed (one second or even less) such that if a user searches using an appropriate keyword, they will be able to see the search results with the updated information.

Near real-time search is the same as that of real-time search, with the difference being the time taken to process the added or modified content. Unlike real-time search, NRT search takes around 30 seconds to process the content, which is even less than one second in case of real-time search. This time period is also called index latency, which is one second or even less for real-time search and approximately 30 seconds in case of NRT.

We will now discuss a few additional information that will definitely help you with its implementation along with handling any challenges you face while implementing. They are as follows:

- Follow guidance for performance tuning especially in terms of schema handling and bulk data-loading in multiple threads.

- It is recommended that you avoid virtualization and implement SSDs if you can afford.

- Adjust the commit rate so that it is prompt enough to satisfy the desired index latency, ensuring that Solr's warming from the previous commit has been accomplished successfully. Usage of `autoCommit` and/or `commitWithin` is recommended.

- Try to keep warming at a minimum as possible. To do so, you may reduce the `autowarmCount` value of your caches and reduce the workload of your queries in the `newSearcher` listener as and when required.

- Try setting `useColdSearcher` to `true` and `maxWarmingSearchers` to `1`.

- In the case of a huge document count, increase the number of shards so that each shard is small, resulting in faster querying. It also helps NRT search due to the fact that smaller shards help balance the effects of slow searches raised by a number of configuration choices.

- Reduce the ratio of the shard count in a machine per CPU cores, enabling a greater number of machines to be available for frequency commits and warming activities.

- Use replication only for backup or disaster-recovery purposes. As you want the indexing and searching to be performed on the same index, it is not recommended to use replication to split the indexing master and the searching slave.

- If you need NRT search only for the added documents and not for the modified ones, I suggest that you index such documents in a small shard (only meant to hold new documents). Due to its light weight (the selected documents are only indexed), it will definitely perform well and will have lower index latency. You might need to merge this into a larger shard occasionally; you may use the `mergeIndexes` core command.

Summary

In this chapter, we mainly concentrated on different techniques to optimize Solr's performance. We started with understanding the various performance factors responsible for Solr's performance and covered vital concepts such as how to replicate an index in a master-slave architecture, and learned more about implementing different Solr-caching techniques such as document caching, query result caching, filter caching, and finally how to cache the whole result page. We also understood SolrCloud and how to perform various activities based on performance optimization, such as creating a SolrCloud cluster, having more than one collection in a SolrCloud cluster, and managing the SolrCloud cluster that you have created or those that already exist. Additionally, we learned how to play around with distributed indexing and searching, which are automated activities carried out on the documents, and how to stop automatic document distribution based on the certain scenarios. By the end of the chapter, we also learned how to get an instance result set using the near real-time search.

In the next chapter, we will scale our performance-optimization techniques and learn more about how to get similar documents based on the rendered result set, and sorting results using function values. We will also learn how to search words based on how they sound, ignoring the predefined words from a search.

4
Additional Performance Optimization Techniques

In the previous chapter, we learned different ways to optimize our Solr's performance, starting from understanding the required factors affecting performance, leading on to advanced concepts such as index replication using the master-slave architecture, Solr caching, SolrCloud, and how to scale your Solr instance horizontally. This means that we learned by playing around with multiple Solr servers and sharding, distributed search, and many more.

In this chapter, we will learn how to optimize performance for a few more activities that are rarely used, such as searching for documents that are similar to the ones returned in the search's result set, sorting results based on a function value (the geospatial search), searching for words that sound alike (that is, searching for homophones), and restricting a word or a list of predefined words (say for example, offensive words) from getting displayed to the end user in the search results. We will cover the following topics:

- Documents similar to those returned in the search result
- Sorting results by function values
- Searching for homophones
- Ignoring the defined words from being searched

So, let us get started.

Documents similar to those returned in the search result

Imagine a situation where you need to search for documents that are similar to those you have searched before using some keywords and have been rendered by Solr as a search result. We will continue with our music composition e-commerce portal that we have been using for demonstration purposes. In this section, we will understand how to get similar documents (in our case, music composition) in the search result along with the result set rendered by the user while searching for a keyword.

Let us start by adding the following index structure to the `fields` section of our `schema.xml` file:

```
<field name="wm_id" type="string" indexed="true" stored="true"
required="true" />
<field name="wm_name" type="text" indexed="true" stored="true"
termVectors="true" />
```

We will use the following example data to work with:

```
<add>
  <doc>
    <field name="wm_id">wm1</field>
    <field name="wm_name">Sonata solo flute</field>
  </doc>
  <doc>
    <field name="wm_id">wm2</field>
    <field name="wm_name">Sonata for string</field>
  </doc>
  <doc>
    <field name="wm_id">wm3</field>
    <field name="wm_name">Quartet for flute</field>
  </doc>
  <doc>
    <field name="wm_id">wm4</field>
    <field name="wm_name">Quartet for string</field>
  </doc>
</add>
```

Let us consider that a user wishes to search for compositions that have `Sonata` and `string` in their names. Moreover, we want the search results to contain compositions not exactly matching but similar to the ones that are returned and exactly match the search criteria. To achieve this, we have sent the following query to our Solr server:

```
http://localhost:8983/solr/select?q=sonata+string&mm=2&qf=wm_name&def
Type=edismax&mlt=true&mlt.fl=wm_name&mlt.mintf=1&mlt.mindf=1
```

The result set returned by our Solr instance for the preceding query is as follows:

```xml
<?xml version="1.0" encoding="UTF-8"?>
<response>
  <lst name="responseHeader">
    <int name="status">0</int>
    <int name="QTime">3</int>
    <lst name="params">
      <str name="mm">2</str>
      <str name="mlt.mindf">1</str>
      <str name="mlt.fl">name</str>
      <str name="q">sonata string</str>
      <str name="mlt.mintf">1</str>
      <str name="qf">wm_name</str>
      <str name="mlt">true</str>
      <str name="defType">edismax</str>
    </lst>
  </lst>
  <result name="response" numFound="1" start="0">
    <doc>
      <str name="wm_id">wm2</str>
      <str name="wm_name">Sonata for string</str>
      <long name="_version_">1234566105364386482</long>
    </doc>
  </result>
<lst name="moreLikeThis">
  <result name="wm3" numFound="3" start="0">
    <doc>
      <str name="wm_id">wm1</str>
      <str name="wm_name">Sonata solo flute</str>
      <long name="_version_">1234566105364387641</long>
    </doc>
    <doc>
      <str name="wm_id">wm4</str>
      <str name="wm_name">Quartet for string</str>
      <long name="_version_">1234566105364390120</long>
    </doc>
    <doc>
      <str name="wm_id">wm3</str>
      <str name="wm_name">Quartet for flute</str>
      <long name="_version_">1234566105364396659</long>
    </doc>
  </result>
</lst>
</response>
```

Let us now understand how it worked!

Firstly, we defined the index structure in the `schema.xml` file with the `field` values as `wm_id` and `wm_name`. You must have noticed that we also used an attribute named `termVectors` and set it as `true` for the `wm_name` field. It is a good practice to use this so as to allow more components similar to this to do their job.

If you look at the query, you will find that we used a few additional parameters with the standard `q` parameter (that is, `mm` and `defType`) to instruct Solr how to handle the query. The `mlt=true` parameter indicates that we would like to consider more components similar to this while processing the result. The `mlt.fl` parameter denotes the field name where we want more components like this to be imposed (in our case, the `wm_name` field). The `mlt.mindf` parameter instructs Solr to ignore the terms from the documents found in the original result set with a term frequency below the specified value. In our case, we don't want the terms that have a frequency less than 1. The last parameter `mlt.mindf` instructs Solr to ignore the documents where the words that appear are less than the defined value. In our case, we considered words that appear in at least one of the documents.

Let us now understand the result set. We can see that we have received an additional line in the response (`<lst name="moreLikeThis">`), which is responsible for showing up the search results associated with more components like this. One more component like this is added to the response for each document found in the search result. In this case, Solr added a section for the document that possesses the unique identifier `wm3` (`<result name="wm3" numFound="3" start="0">`), and the total number of documents found and categorized in this section were 3. You must have also noticed that the value of the `wm_id` attribute has been assigned the value of the unique identifier for the document based on which similar documents have been computed.

Sorting results by function values

Consider a situation where you have an application that stores the list of publishing houses in the index and allows users to search it. Added to the situation, you are more concerned about the publishers that are located near the point where you reside and where you are currently searching the information. In this case, you need some feature that you need to sort your search result based on the distance from a geographical point. Can Solr help you achieve this? The answer is yes, and we will demonstrate how we can achieve it in this section.

This section uses geospatial search. Thus, if you are not familiar with geospatial search, we recommend that you refer to the *Geospatial Search* section covered in *Chapter 1, Searching Data, Administrating Solr, Packt Publishing*.

Let us now start with the actual activity by adding the following index structure in the `fields` section of our `schema.xml` file:

```
<field name="p_id" type="string" indexed="true" stored="true"
required="true" />
<field name="p_name" type="text" indexed="true" stored="true" />
<field name="p_geo" type="location" indexed="true" stored="true" />
<dynamicField p_name="*_coordinate" type="tdouble" indexed="true"
stored="false" />
```

The following is the data we want to index to our Solr instance:

```
<add>
  <doc>
    <field name="p_id">1</field>
    <field name="p_name">Publisher one</field>
    <field name="p_geo">12.5,12.5</field>
  </doc>
  <doc>
    <field name="p_id">2</field>
    <field name="p_name">Publisher two</field>
    <field name="p_geo">15.2,15.2</field>
  </doc>
  <doc>
    <field name="p_id">3</field>
    <field name="p_name">Publisher three</field>
    <field name="p_geo">18.6,18.6</field>
  </doc>
</add>
```

In order to have geospatial search in action, we need to define the following `fieldtype` tag in the `types` section of our `schema.xml` file:

```
<fieldType p_name="location" class="solr.LatLonType" subFieldSuffix="_
coordinate"/>
```

Let us assume that one of the users is accessing their system from a geographical point (20, 20) and searching for the term `publisher`. In order to render the search results that are sorted based on the distance from a given point, we send the following query to our Solr instance:

```
http://localhost:8983/solr/select?q=p_name:company&sort=geodist(geo,2
0,20)+asc
```

The rendered search result set is as follows:

```xml
<?xml version="1.0" encoding="UTF-8"?>
<response>
<lst name="responseHeader">
<int name="status">0</int>
<int name-"QTime">3</int>
<lst name="params">
<str name="q">p_name:publisher</str>
<str name="sort">geodist(geo,20,20) asc</str>
</lst>
</lst>
<result name="response" numFound="3" start="0">
<doc>
<str name="p_id">3</str>
<str name="p_name">Publisher three</str>
<str name="p_geo">18.6,18.6</str>
</doc>
<doc>
<str name="p_id">2</str>
<str name="p_name">Publisher two</str>
<str name="p_geo">15.2,15.2</str>
</doc>
<doc>
<str name="p_id">1</str>
<str name="p_name">Publisher one</str>
<str name="p_geo">12.5,12.5</str>
</doc>
</result>
</response>
```

As you can see in the preceding response, our query worked perfectly! So, let us now understand what we did and why.

We started by defining the index structure in schema.xml. We defined four fields, the p_id field to hold the unique identifier, the p_name field to hold the name of the publishing house, the p_geo field to hold the geographical location of each publishing house, and the last field, which is dynamic in nature and needs the location field type to function. We will skip the discussion about our example data as it is very simple to understand.

Apart from the standard `q` parameter, we have also used the `sort` parameter, which functions a bit different from the one you probably might be used to. We have used the `geodist` function with the `sort` parameter because this function calculates the distance from a given geographical point and queues the result for the sorting activity. The first argument that we used with the `geodist` function is `geo`, which specifies the field to be used to compute the distance. The next two arguments (in our case, `20`, `20`) denote the geographical point that the distance needs to be calculated from. To instruct the sort order, we have used the `asc` value to get the result list sorted in ascending order. If you want to have the sort order based on the larger distance first, you need to use `desc` instead of `asc`.

Searching for homophones

You might encounter end users whose English is not that good, so they type the search keywords either as they sound or the way they are pronounced. For instance, words such as break and brake, meat and meet, tale and tail, and phone and fone sound the same when pronounced. There might be situations where the end user might intend to search for phone, and due to certain reasons, they type `fone`. In such a scenario, by default, Solr considers `fone` (the word actually typed by the user) instead of phone (what the user actually meant), and the relevant documents are prone to be missed in the rendered result set. To avoid missing the relevant documents in the search results, we need to handle this in such a way that our Solr should be capable of rendering the results for the keywords that sound similar to the typed ones. Can such scenarios be handled by our Solr? The answer is yes; we can make our Solr capable of performing well, and we will learn how to do it in this section.

In our demonstration, we will consider the word pair phone and fone.

Let us start by defining the following index structure in the `fields` section of our `schema.xml` file:

```
<field name="h_id" type="string" indexed="true" stored="true"
required="true" />
<field name="h_name" type="phonetic" indexed="true" stored="true" />
```

Now, we will define the `phonetic` field type in the `types` section of our `schema.xml` file by adding the following code snippet:

```
<fieldType name="phonetic" stored="false" indexed="true" class="solr.
TextField" >
  <analyzer>
    <tokenizer class="solr.StandardTokenizerFactory"/>
    <filter class="solr.DoubleMetaphoneFilterFactory" inject="false"/>
  </analyzer>
</fieldType>
```

We have the following example data that we will need to index:

```
<add>
  <doc>
    <field name="h_id">1</field>
    <field name="h_name">Fone</field>
  </doc>
  <doc>
    <field name="h_id">2</field>
    <field name="h_name">Phone</field>
  </doc>
  <doc>
    <field name="h_id">3</field>
    <field name="h_name">Mohan</field>
  </doc>
</add>
```

Assuming that our end user is interested in finding the documents that sounds like `fon`, we send the following query:

```
http://localhost:8983/solr/select?q=h_name:fon
```

We get the following response:

```
<?xml version="1.0" encoding="UTF-8"?>
<response>
  <lst name="responseHeader">
    <int name="status">0</int>
    <int name="QTime">2</int>
    <lst name="params">
      <str name="q">h_name:fon</str>
    </lst>
  </lst>
<result name="response" numFound="2" start="0">
  <doc>
    <str name="h_id">1</str>
    <str name="h_name">Fone</str>
  </doc>
  <doc>
    <str name="h_id">2</str>
    <str name="h_name">Phone</str>
  </doc>
</result>
</response>
```

If you notice the preceding response, you will find that two documents have been rendered that sound like `fon`, and one of the documents that sounds far different from `fon` has been omitted. Now, let us understand how it worked.

We defined the index structure in our `schema.xml` file with `h_id` as the unique identifier field and the `h_name` field to hold the name, which looked quite simple. Thus, we will skip its explanation.

In our example, the `h_name` field is the one based on which the phonetic search has been applied to. In order to apply phonetic search, we have defined a new field `type` as `phonetic`. Apart from the standard class and others, we have also defined a new filter `DoubleMetaphoneFilterFactory`, which is responsible for investigating how the word or a set of words sound using double metaphone to do its job. We have used the `inject="false"` attribute to instruct Solr to replace the original tokens with the ones produced by the filter.

As you can see in our query and data, the `fon` word matched two words (that is, `phone` and `fone`), and the left one word unmatched (that is, `Mohan`). This means that our algorithm and the filter worked perfectly!

> If you are keen to learn other phonetic algorithms, I recommend that you refer to the Solr Wiki page at `http://wiki.apache.org/solr/AnalyzersTokenizersTokenFilters`.

Ignore the defined words from being searched

Imagine a situation where you wish to filter out offensive words from the indexed data. Such words need to be ignored and shouldn't be searchable. Can we provide such a capability to Solr? Yes, of course; we can do that and we will understand how to do it in this section.

In order to avoid using offensive words in the demonstration, we will use the term `offensive`, which denotes any offensive word we would like to filter out from being searched.

In order to start, we will define the following index structure in the `fields` section of our `schema.xml` file:

```
<field name="o_id" type="string" indexed="true" stored="true"
required="true" />
<field name="o_name" type="text_offensive" indexed="true"
stored="true" />
```

Now, let us define the `text_offensive` field type in the `types` section of our `schema.xml` file as follows:

```
<fieldType name="text_offensive" class="solr.TextField"
positionIncrementGap="100">
  <analyzer>
    <tokenizer class="solr.WhitespaceTokenizerFactory"/>
    <filter class="solr.StopFilterFactory" ignoreCase="true"
words="offensive.txt" enablePositionIncrements="true" />
  </analyzer>
</fieldType>
```

We have now created the `offensive.txt` file (mentioned in the preceding code snippet), and placed it in the same directory as that of `schema.xml` with the following content that you want to filter out from the search results:

offensive

offensive1

offensive2

offensive3

offensive4

Let us index our example data as follows:

```
<add>
  <doc>
    <field name="o_id">1</field>
    <field name="o_name">Surendra</field>
  </doc>
  <doc>
    <field name="o_id">2</field>
    <field name="o_name">Mohan</field>
  </doc>
</add>
```

Let us assume that the user wishes to find the documents that consist of the words `Mohan` and `offensive`. Thus, the query that we send to Solr looks as follows:

```
http://localhost:8983/solr/select?q=o_name:(Mohan+AND+offensive)
```

Based on the data that we indexed, in a standard situation we won't expect any document to be rendered due to the fact that we don't have any indexed document that matches both the keywords `Mohan` and `offensive`. Some magic happened and Solr returns the following response:

```xml
<?xml version="1.0" encoding="UTF-8"?>
<response>
<lst name="responseHeader">
<int name="status">0</int>
<int name="QTime">2</int>
<lst name="params">
<str name="q">o_name:(Mohan AND offensive)</str>
</lst>
</lst>
<result name="response" numFound="1" start="0">
<doc>
<str name="o_id">2</str>
<str name="o_name">Mohan</str>
</doc>
</result>
</response>
```

It was able to find a document instead of none; we can infer that our query worked perfectly by ignoring the term we wanted to filter out from our search results. Let us now understand how it worked.

We defined the o_id and o_name fields in the schema.xml file that holds a unique identifier and name, respectively. Since it is a simple definition, we will skip the explanation and proceed to the next one.

We have applied Solr's StopFilterFactory filter on the o_name field in order to ignore the offensive words. We also defined the text_offensive field type, and it is analyzed in the default manner. Let us concentrate on the StopFilterFactory filter that we have used here. We used the words attribute for this filter, which states the name of the encoded UTF-8 file, which holds the list of words (one word per line) that need to be ignored while searching and should be placed in the same directory as that of our schema.xml file. The ignoreCase="true" parameter instructs the filter to process the offensive words and tokens irrespective of the case used to define in the file (offensive.txt), that is, process it in a case-insensitive manner. The enablePositionIncrements="true" parameter enables Solr to increment the position of the tokens in the token stream.

As you can see from the query, we instructed Solr to search for the documents that contain both the Mohan and offensive words (using the AND operator); this means that we expect both the words to be present in the documents that have been rendered in the result set. However, this is not the case as we didn't get any document containing the word offensive. This is because we instructed Solr to ignore all the words listed in the offensive.txt file, resulting in the documents we expected.

Summary

In this chapter, we covered rarely used but important techniques to optimize the performance of our Solr instance, learned more about how to get similar documents based on the rendered result set, what is the geospatial search (search documents with respect to a specific geographical point), how to search for words based on how they sound, and how to ignore the predefined words from getting searched.

In the next chapter, we will learn how to troubleshoot common problems that are not limited to dealing with corrupted and locked indexes, how to truncate the index size and tackle issues caused due to expensive garbage collections, out-of-memory, and infinite loop execution while playing around with shards.

5
Troubleshooting

You must have faced a number of problems while playing around with Solr's deployment, irrespective of whether the deployment is simple or complex, or whether you are working on a single Solr instance or multiple servers or shards.

In this chapter, we will learn how to troubleshoot a list of the most common problems you are prone to facing while you are still in the Solr playground, and will cover the following topics:

- Dealing with the corrupt index
- Reducing the file count in the index
- Dealing with the locked index
- Truncating the index size
- Dealing with a huge count of open files
- Dealing with out-of-memory issues
- Dealing with an infinite loop exception in shards
- Dealing with expensive garbage collection
- Bulk updating a single field without full indexation

So, let us get started.

Dealing with the corrupt index

Assume that you are maintaining a Solr instance, and suddenly, probably at late midnight, you are informed that the index is corrupted and you need to investigate and fix the issue at the earliest. Imagine how frustrating it is to address such priority issues, that too at midnight! You might be wondering whether there is an alternative to full indexation or restoring the working index from the backup. Yes, we do have alternatives to full indexation and/or restoring to the backup that won't consume excess time compared to the preceding options, and we will learn how to do it in this section.

Assuming that we have a corrupt index that we need to investigate and fix, we will have to switch the working directory to the one holding Lucene libraries in order to use the `CheckIndex` tool. On switching to the appropriate directory, run the following command:

```
java -cp JAR_PATH_LUCENE -ea:org.apache.lucene...org.apache.lucene.index.
CheckIndex PATH_INDEX -fix
```

In the preceding command, `JAR_PATH_LUCENE` is the path to Lucene libraries (in our case, `/solr/lucene`), and `PATH_INDEX` is the path to the index (in our case, `/usr/share/solr/data/index`).

Thus, in our case, the actual command would be as follows:

```
java -cp /solr/lucene/lucene-core-4.6-SNAPSHOT.jar -ea:org.apache.
lucene... org.apache.lucene.index.CheckIndex /usr/share/solr/data/
index -fix
```

As a response to the command, we find the list of processes associated to the index repair, as shown in the following screenshot:

```
Opening index @ C:Solrsolrdataindex
Segments file=segments_1 numSegments=1 version=FORMAT_DIAGNOSTICS [Lucene
4.6]
1 of 1: name=_0 docCount=39
compound=false
hasProx=true
numFiles=39
size (MB)=0,917
diagnostics = {os.version=6.1, os=Windows 7, lucene.version=4.6.0
- 2014-01-06 12:58:52, source=flush, os.arch=x86, java.version=1.7.0_45,
java.vendor=Sun Microsystems Inc.}
no deletions
test: open reader.........FAILED
WARNING: fixIndex() would remove reference to this segment; full
exception:
org.apache.lucene.index.CorruptIndexException: did not read all bytes
from file "_0.fnm": read 154 vs size 158
at org.apache.lucene.index.FieldInfos.read(FieldInfos.java:370)
at org.apache.lucene.index.FieldInfos.<init>(FieldInfos.java:71)
at org.apache.lucene.index.SegmentReader$CoreReaders.<init>(SegmentRead
er.java:119)
at org.apache.lucene.index.SegmentReader.get(SegmentReader.java:652)
at org.apache.lucene.index.SegmentReader.get(SegmentReader.java:605)
at org.apache.lucene.index.CheckIndex.checkIndex(CheckIndex.java:491)
at org.apache.lucene.index.CheckIndex.main(CheckIndex.java:903)
WARNING: 1 broken segment (containing 39 documents) detected
WARNING: 39 documents will be lost
NOTE: will write new segments file in 8 seconds; this will remove 39 docs
from the index. THIS IS YOUR LAST CHANCE TO CTRL+C!
5...
4...
3...
2...
1...
Writing...
OK
Wrote new segments file "segments_2"
```

This is how we investigated the corrupt index and proceeded to its repair activity. Now, let us understand how we achieved our purpose.

If you refer to the command, you will find that we have executed the `CheckIndex` class shipped with the `apache.lucene.index` bundle and passed parameters such as the absolute path to the directory holding the index files, the path to Lucene containing the required library files, and the `-fix` parameter that instructs `CheckIndex` to attempt fixing any bugs found in the index structure. Additionally, we passed the `ea` parameter in order to activate assertion, which helps the testing process to be more accurate.

As a response, we can see the information about the segments, document count, the Lucene version used to build the index, OS information, and so on. Since this information is not crucial to us, we may skip to the following piece of response:

```
WARNING: 1 broken segment (containing 39 documents) detected
WARNING: 39 documents will be lost
```

The preceding piece of response denotes that we have found one broken segment containing `39` documents, with a warning that all these documents will be lost during the repair process. Though, this is not always the case; however, it is always recommended to be alert to handle the repair in case the documents are really lost.

As soon as the broken segment and the associated documents were found, the `CheckIndex` tool started writing new segment files, which are the repaired ones. That's all! In case of a larger index, it is highly expected that the `CheckIndex` response you receive is a huge one that contains information about all the segments. Since we have considered a simple example, we got a handful of responses, but this is usually not the case.

You might come across situations where you are not able to repair the index using the `CheckIndex` tool that resulted in index deletion while attempting to repair that index. Thus, it is always recommended that you take the latest index backup before you attempt to repair it.

Moreover, if you are interested in checking the errors in the index without being interested in fixing them, you may still run the `CheckIndex` tool, but without the `-fix` option. Your command would be as follows:

```
java -ea:org.apache.lucene... org.apache.lucene.index.
CheckIndex /usr/share/solr/data/index
```

Reducing the file count in the index

Consider a situation where you have a Solr instance running for a long duration and the index is split into multiple files (which is quite natural and expected). Did you imagine how time-consuming it is for Solr to keep connecting all the files of an index to fetch the desired result set, resulting in a performance drop? Don't get hassled; we can figure this out and we will learn how to overcome the issue in this section.

Since the root cause behind this performance drop is the segment's file count (which is huge) that is associated to an index, the solution we can think of is to find a way to merge these split off segment files into one. To do so, we run the `optimize` command as follows:

```
curl 'http://localhost:8983/solr/update' --data-binary '<optimize/>' -H
'Content-type:text/xml; charset=utf-8'
```

After a couple of minutes or probably hours (this primarily depends on the index size), you will get the following response:

```
<?xml version="1.0" encoding="UTF-8"?>
<response>
  <lst name="responseHeader">
    <int name="status">0</int>
    <int name="QTime">95387</int>
  </lst>
    <str name="WARNING">This response format is experimental. It is
likely to change in the future.</str>
</response>
```

Our motive behind using the `optimize` command is that we wanted to create a new segment file with the contents of all the older segment files and then delete them. During the execution of this command, you might notice that the size of the index gets doubled. This is because while the segment files are merged into the newly created one, the older segment files are not removed, thus increasing the index size. Let the command run, and by the end of its execution, you will notice that the size of the index is back to normal or even smaller.

We have used the `curl` command to trigger the `optimize` command as we are using a Unix-based environment. Since we have used the `curl` command for the purpose of sending requests, you may achieve this even by using HTTP POST or the SolrJ library based on the environment (in terms of the operating system) that you use.

It is a good practice to trigger the optimize command once a day or probably once every alternate day. But before you set the time period, keep in mind that the optimize command extensively uses I/O operations when in action. Thus, it is recommended that you trigger optimize only in off-peak hours, on the master server too. Moreover, don't forget to trigger this command on each and every core you have in your Solr server.

Dealing with the locked index

Imagine a situation where, while the indexing process was active, something went wrong, probably your machine crashed or a problem occurred in your virtual machine, resulting in index locking. Let me remind you that when indexing is in progress, it locks the current file in the index directory. When this process aborts abruptly due to certain reasons, the file that is already locked remains as it is, restricting the modification of the index. Our motive would be to sort out this locking issue, and we will learn how to do it in this section.

Let us assume that during the commit operation, our Java Virtual Machine crashed and an intern killed our Solr master instance while the indexing was in progress. The Jetty servlet container normally throws an exception, which looks as follows:

```
SEVERE: Exception during commit/optimize:java.io.IOException: Lock obtain
timed out: SimpleFSLock@/usr/share/solr/data/index/luceneff1fe872c2cbfeb4
4091b36c21a97c14-write.lock
```

If you are sure that there is no indexing process currently running, navigate to the /usr/share/solr/data/index directory, and here you will find the culprit with the name luceneff1fe872c2cbfeb44091b36c21a97c14-write.lock. Delete this file and restart Jetty, and the problem is solved!

Let us understand how it worked. During the commit operation, we found that our virtual machine crashed, resulting in an exception. This exception stated that a lock has occurred and it shares a filename along with its location (a file in the lucene-*-write.lock format) for us to take the appropriate action. Since this file was the locked one, we were not able to modify our index. Thus, we decided to delete this file so that our index is unlocked. We then restarted Jetty, which triggers this unlock activity to action.

Truncating the index size

You might come across situations where you need to truncate the index size to such an extent that it fits into your system's RAM. We will learn how to truncate the index size to a desirable level in this section.

Let us consider our music composition `eStore` for the demonstration purposes. Assuming that we have four fields that describe the document, we will add the following index structure to the `fields` section of our `schema.xml` file:

```
<field name="wm_id" type="string" indexed="true" stored="true"
required="true" />
<field name="wm_name" type="text" indexed="true" stored="true" />
<field name="wm_details" type="text" indexed="true" stored="true" />
<field name="wm_price" type="string" indexed="true" stored="true" />
```

We will also assume the following points:

- Search is to be carried out in the `wm_name` and `wm_details` fields
- We show the `wm_id` and `wm_price` fields
- We restrict Solr from using spellchecker and highlighting

We indexed 2,000,000 example documents based on the preceding index structure and recorded the index size as 769,344,201 bytes.

Now, we will make the following changes to our index structure:

- Set the `stored` attribute to `false` for the `wm_name` and `wm_details` fields, which was set as `true` earlier
- Set the `indexed` attribute to `false` for the `wm_price` field, which was `true` earlier
- Add the options `termVectors="false"`, `termPositions="false"`, and `termOffsets="false"` to the fields `wm_name` and `wm_details`

On following the preceding guidelines, our modified index structure would look as follows:

```
<field name="wm_id" type="string" indexed="true" stored="true"
required="true" />
<field name="wm_name" type="text" indexed="true" stored="false"
termVectors="false" termPositions="false" termOffsets="false"/>
<field name="wm_details" type="text" indexed="true" stored="false"
termVectors="false" termPositions="false" termOffsets="false"/>
<field name="wm_price" type="string" indexed="false" stored="true" />
```

Then we indexed the same documents using this modified index structure and found that the index size has been reduced to 219,812,629 bytes. Doesn't the new index size look amazing!

Let us now understand how it worked.

We defined our index structure for our sample document in `schema.xml` that consists of four fields. Since the definition is a basic one, we will not cover this in detail.

Since our intention was to search only based on the wm_name and wm_details fields, we don't want the wm_price field to be indexed. Thus, we set the indexed attribute as false for the wm_price field, thus saving the index size. The indexed="false" attribute instructs Solr not to index the specific field(s) that are associated with this attribute. The stored attribute needs to be set as true only when we are obliged to show the specific field(s) in the search results, else it is a good practice to set it as false, which helps reducing the index size to a marginal extent. The stored="false" attribute instructs Solr not to store this field's original value. Doing this also excludes this field from being present in the search results.

Since one of our requirements was to avoid the use of the spellchecker and highlighting features, we were able to reduce the index size even further by appending termVector="false", termPositions="false", and termOffsets ="false" to the wm_name and wm_details fields. These attributes instruct Solr to not store any information that is associated with these terms, thereby saving another slot of index size.

> In order to reduce the index size, first go for the optimization and then look into your schema.xml file to understand whether you really need all the fields. Then list down the fields you don't want to be stored and/ or indexed along with whether you need the term information, and apply the preceding steps accordingly.

Dealing with a huge count of open files

In this section, we will learn how to get rid of exceptions thrown due to a huge number of files that are open. Before you get into this section, it is recommended that you refer to one of the preceding sections called *Reducing the file count in the index*.

1. For the purpose of demonstration, let us assume that Solr (running on a Unix environment) throws the exception whose header looks as follows:

    `java.io.FileNotFoundException: /use/share/solr/data/index/_8.tii`

    This shows that there are too many open files.

2. We will increase the opened files' limit from 1000 (this was earlier set in my case, and is prone to differ) to 3000. To do so, we will use the ulimit command-line utility as follows:

    `ulimit -n 3000`

3. Stopping at this stage would just prove to be a workaround. The primary cause behind this exception is the huge number of segment files that constitute an index. So, the immediate activity proceeding with the `ulimit` utility should be to optimize the index. We recommend that you follow the guidelines discussed in the *Reducing the file count in the index* section.

4. Now, let us set the `mergeFactor` section to a lower value, say 2. We choose a lower value for `mergeFactor` because the lower its value, the fewer files will be used to build the index, and vice versa. So, we alter the `mergeFactor` section in our `solrconfig.xml` file and set it as 2 (as shown in the following code):

```
<mergeFactor>2</mergeFactor>
```

5. If doing so doesn't serve our purpose, we will activate the `compound` index structure. In order to enable this, we add the following line of code to our `solrconfig.xml` file:

```
<useCompoundFile>true</useCompoundFile>
```

6. Once it's done, we run the index optimization, and that's it!

Now let us understand what we did.

- We used the `ulimit` command-line utility to set the maximum number of files we want to be opened concurrently.

- Next, we used the `mergeFactor` configuration utility that defines the segment file count. In our case, we have set `mergeFactor` as 2, which is quite a low value compared to the default one (which is 10).

- Moving to the last component, that is, `useCompoundFile`, which we have set as `true`. This setting activates the `compound` index structure and instructs Solr to use this structure to the maximum extent, thus reducing the number of files that contribute in creating an index.

While altering the `mergeFactor` value, we recommend that you keep a couple of things in mind. Firstly, the lower the value of `mergeFactor` is, the longer the indexing time will be. Hence, it enhances the search speed to a greater extent. On the contrary, the higher the value is, the quicker the indexing process is. However, search time is prone to degrade due to the fact that the index is built of a larger number of files.

Dealing with out-of-memory issues

You might be aware that every application written in Java is well known for out-of-memory problems. Before we learn how to deal with the out-of-memory problems, let us define out-of-memory in Java terms and briefly understand why such problems occur. It is defined as the state of a Java machine where no additional memory can be allocated to run a process that is in progress. This results in the denial of transferring additional data into the memory, which is essential to run a process appropriately, thereby leading to a cease of the process. We recommend that you refer to the out-of-memory Wiki page at `http://en.wikipedia.org/wiki/Out_of_memory` if you want to know more about it.

As far as Solr is concerned, these problems are usually associated with a low heap size. We will learn how to avoid and resolve such problems in this section.

You might come across an exception that looks similar to the following one:

`SEVERE: java.lang.OutOfMemoryError: Java heap space`

The first thing that comes in our mind is to allocate additional memory to our Java-based virtual machine. In order to do so, we add the Xmx parameter and set the Xms parameter to run during the start of our servlet container (Tomcat, Jetty, and so on). To do so, run the following command:

`java -Xmx2048M -Xms512m -jar start.jar`

Since this is just the initial step, by the end of the day you will probably have figured out the expensive documents and tried to reduce Solr's memory usage. Firstly, investigate your index to see if all the files are there in place. Also, ensure that each and every field that builds the documents has been dwelt in the memory.

Now, it is time to look at our queries to investigate how they have been built, how the faceting mechanism is being executed, and so on and so forth. For example, `facet.method=fc` consumes less memory when a field has a number of distinct terms associated to it in the index.

Out-of-heap memory may also occur when you attempt to fetch too many documents at a time. This situation is very similar to setting a larger value for the query result window. Additionally, you may run out of memory when you attempt calculating too many faceting results. Thus, it is always recommended that you have a comparatively lower value for the query result window and avoid complex faceted calculations. You may also investigate the cache size as this may also be one of the culprits of the out-of-memory exception.

Now, let us understand what we did. Basically, we used the Xmx and Xms parameters to achieve our purpose. The Xms parameter denotes the heap memory size, which we want the virtual machine to use at the start. Hence, this value is the minimum heap memory size that the virtual machine will use. On the other hand, the Xmx parameter denotes the maximum heap memory size that a virtual machine can use.

To summarize, Xms and Xmx are limits to the heap memory size that can be used by our virtual machine.

> Sometimes, it is good to set the same value for the Xms and Xmx parameters. This will ensure that our virtual machine doesn't invest its precious time and resources in resizing the heap size.

The preceding guidelines are capable enough to resolve the out-of-memory issue. Despite following the preceding steps if the issue crops up again, we recommend that you start monitoring your heap. The most convenient way we can think of to monitor our heap is to use the most appropriate virtual machine parameters. They are XX:+HeapDumpOnOutOfMemory and XX:HeapDumpPath. These two parameters instruct Solr to dump the heap on the out-of-memory exception and write a log to a file created in a specific directory. To apply this, we will run the default Solr deployment start command, which is as follows:

```
java -jar -XX:+HeapDumpOnOutOfMemoryError -XX:HeapDumpPath=/logs/
Memorylog/ start.jar
```

Dealing with an infinite loop exception in shards

As you might be aware that while working with shards, we need to add the IP address of the shards to every query we shoot. To avoid including the IP address of the shards on every query, something might come to mind and you suddenly think of writing them to solrconfig.xml and leave the task of adding the shards' addresses to Solr. So, you added them to the default request handler of your solrconfig.xml file and executed your example query that landed in an infinite loop exception. You might be wondering how to prevent such exceptions from occurring, despite adding the shard addresses to the handler. In this section, we will learn how to overcome infinite loop exception in shards.

We define the following request handler in our solrconfig.xml file, assuming that the IP address of the Solr server we are going to query is 192.168.0.100:

```
<requestHandler name="standard" class="solr.SearchHandler"
default="true">
```

```
<lst name="defaults">
  <str name="shards">192.168.0.100:8983/solr,192.168.0.101:8983/
solr,192.168.0.102:8983</str>
</lst>
</requestHandler>
```

Now, we sent our example query to this handler, and on executing the query, we landed in an infinite loop exception. With the motive of avoiding such an exception, we added a new handler instead of adding the shards to the default one. Our new request handler's definition in `solrconfig.xml` is as follows:

```
<requestHandler name="excshards" class="solr.SearchHandler">
<lst name="defaults">
  <str name="shards">192.168.0.100:8983/solr,192.168.0.101:8983/
solr,192.168.0.102:8983</str>
</lst>
</requestHandler>
```

Now, we want to send the queries that should use shards; we use the new search handler with the name `excshards` instead of the default one. Let us now understand how it worked.

Before we get into the actuals, let us understand what caused this exception. We queried the shards, and Solr considered the default request handler (the default behavior). So when the shard tried to fetch the results, it used the handler containing the shard's definition (in our case, the default request handler got triggered). Thus, it tried to query the shards again and again, resulting in an infinite loop exception.

Later, we defined our shards in a new request handler (`excshards`), which is non-default in nature. We sent our example query to this new handler. Then, the shard mechanism used the default handler to fetch us the results. This time, we didn't face any infinite loop exception, due to the fact that this time we didn't have any shard-related information in the default search handler, which prevented it to get into the infinite loop exception again.

Dealing with expensive garbage collection

You might encounter situations where you have a number of applications running in the Java Virtual Machine and the garbage collection process takes too long to run. Even though this issue occurs, probably you might not be aware of what exactly is happening. In this section, we will learn how to deal with such garbage collections that take too long to execute.

We start by running the following command:

```
java -Xmx2048M -Xms512m -jar start.jar
```

After a certain time period, we noticed that Solr starts to hang frequently for a shorter time period and doesn't even respond during this time span, and it is the same with Jetty. This abnormal behavior of responding and not responding is an indication that our garbage collection is taking too long to execute. How are we going to overcome this issue?

Let us modify our Solr start command and see what happens. Now our command looks as follows:

```
java -Xmx2048M -Xms512m -XX:+UseConcMarkSweepGC -XX:+UseParNewGC
-XX:ParallelGCThreads=6 -XX:SurvivorRatio=3 -jar start.jar
```

Later, we ran a test and noticed that this worked! Now, let us understand how it worked.

We included some magical parameters to our start command that helped us overcome this issue. They are as follows:

- `-XX:+UseConcMarkSweepGC`: This parameter instructs our Java Virtual Machine to concurrently run the old generation garbage collections. This also means that the concurrent mark-sweep collection for the old generation will be activated.
- `-XX:+UseParNewGC`: This parameter activates parallel garbage collection for the young generation.
- `-XX:ParallelGCThreads`: This parameter defines the number of threads we want to be used to perform the garbage-collection activity on the young generation. In our case, we wanted six such threads to be available for this job.
- `-XX:SurvivorRatio`: This parameter defines the ratio of survivor heap space out of the total heap space that we want Solr to use before the objects are pushed to the old generation. In our case, we want one-third of the space to be allocated to the survivor heap space.

 Tuning a Java Virtual Machine is not always useful. Sometimes, adding memory using the Xmx parameter solves our purpose.

Our magical parameters did their jobs appropriately. But it is recommended that we cross-check whether it was really the garbage collector causing problems or if it was something else. To monitor this, we will use `-Xloggc:gc.log` added in the start command. This parameter will log the output coming out of the garbage collector to the `gc.log` file. Now, our initial start command is as follows:

```
java -Xmx2048M -Xms512m -Xloggc:gc.log -jar start.jar
```

Bulk updating a single field without full indexation

You might be aware that if you wish to update a field in a document that is written in the index, in the standard manner, Solr won't allow you. Instead, you need to remove the complete document from the index and add a new version to it. For a smaller index, the standard approach is quite fine. But think of a situation where you have a huge index and you need to update a field that tracks the visitor count hitting the product.

As a standard approach, it is as good as a full indexation of all the documents (probably millions of documents on a daily basis). Do you think full indexation in such a scenario is an optimal approach? Of course not, due to the fact that it is going to utilize ample resources and is better to be avoided. So, how does one handle such a situation? Don't worry! In this section, we will learn how to update a single field in a document without any need for an expensive, complete indexation.

We will refer to our music composition `estore` example for demonstration purposes. Let us assume that our document constitutes of three fields and the index structure looks as follows (added to our `schema.xml` file):

```
<field name="wm_id" type="string" indexed="true" stored="true"
required="true" />
<field name="wm_name" type="text" indexed="true" stored="true" />
<field name="wm_visits" type="visitsWM" />
```

Now, let us define the two field types by adding the following code in the `types` section of our `schema.xml` file:

```
<fieldType name="floatWM" class="solr.FloatField" omitNorms="true"/>
<fieldType name="visitsWM" keyField="wm_id" defVal="0"
stored="false" indexed="false" class="solr.ExternalFileField"
valType="floatWM" />
```

Our test data looks as follows:

```
<add>
  <doc>
    <field name="wm_id">1</field>
    <field name="wm_name">Symphony in C major</field>
  </doc>
  <doc>
    <field name="wm_id">2</field>
    <field name="wm_name">Symphony no 11</field>
  </doc>
  <doc>
    <field name="wm_id">3</field>
    <field name="wm_name">Three owl songs</field>
  </doc>
</add>
```

As you might have noticed, we didn't include the wm_visits field data. Now, let us create a file named external_wm_visits that holds the following information, and place it in the same directory where your index directory resides:

```
1=300
2= 70
3=180
```

Once we start Solr, in order to use the data that we have included in the external_wm_visits file in the boost function, we run the following query that works perfectly:

http://localhost:8983/solr/select?q=wmusic&bf=log(wm_visits)&qt=dismax

Now, let us understand how it worked.

We defined the index structure with three fields, wm_id, wm_name, and wm_visits. We will not go into more detail as the structure is quite simple.

You must have noticed that we have not defined the wm_visits field as the standard field type. Instead, it is based on the visitsWM field type, which is in turn based on solr.ExternalFieldType. This field type permits Solr to fetch records from an external file source, and needs to satisfy the following criteria:

- The external file needs to reside in the same directory as that of the index. For instance, if the path to the index is ~/data/index, then this external file must be placed in the ~/data directory.

- The nomenclature of the file should be in the external_FIELDNAME format. Thus, in our case, the filename is external_wm_visits.

- The data in the file is limited to be used in function queries only.

Now, let us understand the additional attributes we used with the `visitsWM` field type. The `keyField` attribute stated that the field in the index should hold the unique identifier of the document. The `defVal` attribute is denoted by the default value that the field should hold. The last attribute, that is, `valType`, stated the type of data that resides in the external field. In our case, we defined the `floatWM` field type, which is based on `solr.FloatField`, accepted by Solr for `solr.ExternalFieldType`.

As you can see in our example data, we didn't include the visits-related information in the standard file; instead, we stated this information in the `external_wm_visits` file. The structure of the file is quite simple. We stated each entry in a specific pattern, that is, a unique identifier, a `=` character, and an associated field value. In our case, say for example, `1=300`, the unique identifier is `1` and will hold the field value of `300`.

> There are a couple of more things you should understand while playing around with external fields. Firstly, you can't play around with the data from the external file for searching, sorting, displaying, and other activities. It can be only used as a value to the function query. Secondly, in case there is any kind of modification done on the file, you need to run the `commit` command and then Solr will reload the file content for further use.

Summary

In this chapter, we learned how to troubleshoot common problems and also covered how to deal with corrupted and locked indexes, reducing the number of files in the index, and how to truncate the index size. We also learned how to tackle issues caused due to expensive garbage collections, out-of-memory, too many opened files, infinite loop execution while playing around with shards, and how to update a single field in all documents without full indexation activity.

In the next chapter, we will learn how to use ZooKeeper for performance-optimization purposes and will cover how to set up, configure, and deploy ZooKeeper. We will also understand the different applications of ZooKeeper that can help us optimize our Solr's performance.

6
Performance Optimization with ZooKeeper

In this chapter, we will learn about ZooKeeper and will discuss how to set up, configure, and deploy ZooKeeper in an intention to optimize our Solr's performance. We will also discuss the various applications of ZooKeeper. We will cover the following topics:

- Introduction to ZooKeeper
- Setting up, configuring, and deploying ZooKeeper
- Applications of ZooKeeper

So, let us get started.

Getting familiar with ZooKeeper

Let us start with understanding the background of ZooKeeper. When you think of implementing a distributed system across Solr servers and shards, ZooKeeper becomes a mandatory tool.

Prerequisites for a distributed server

In order to design a distributed system, you basically think of designing and developing the following coordination services:

- **Name service**: It is a service that maps an entity to some other information associated to that entity. Assuming that we have an e-commerce online portal named `eStore` consisting of Piano XYZ as one of the products, the name service `eStore` will map Piano XYZ with its other information such as its SKU. In terms of infrastructure management, it is as good as a domain name being mapped to its respective IP address using the DNS service. Since you are going to play around with multiple servers while implementing the distributed system, you should be keeping an eye on which servers and services are currently running and monitor the status based on their names. ZooKeeper will help you facilitate with an interface to do so. It may also extend your name service to be implemented at a group level. This means that you can even associate a specific product category, for instance, to the product information such as product name and SKU.

- **Locking**: It is used to permit serialized access to shared resources in a distributed environment. This may lead to the implementation of distributed mutex (mutual exclusion) so as to ensure that no two or more processes or threads are simultaneously in their critical zone. ZooKeeper facilitates implementing this in a more convenient way.

- **Synchronization**: When you implement a distributed mutex, synchronizing access to the shared resources is a must. To handle synchronization, ZooKeeper provides an easy-to-use interface.

- **Leader election**: You might come across scenarios where the nodes might go offline abruptly and your distribution environment would demand an automated disaster recovery plan. You may achieve this using ZooKeeper through leader election. If you wish to explore more about leader election, you may refer to its Wiki page at http://en.wikipedia.org/wiki/Leader_election.

- **Configuration management**: You can also use ZooKeeper to handle configuration management activities by centralizing and managing the configuration of your distributed system. This also means that if you have created a new node, it will inherit the configuration of the centralized system itself with the help of ZooKeeper.

You have enough flexibility to design and implement all the preceding services from scratch. However, doing so proves to be quite expensive in terms of the overhead of performing extra work, and you might struggle to debug problems, deadlocks, and/or race conditions. Moreover, if you go for hacking a simple group membership service, you may commence it quite easily. But when it comes to writing for reliability, scalability, replication, and other features, it might lead to frustration as it needs a lot more work. To overcome such frustrating workload and provide ease to the developers, Apache ZooKeeper comes into play, which was developed and declared as open source and acts as a scalable, reliable, and high-performance coordination service to the distributed system.

Aid your distributed system using ZooKeeper

The following are a few properties that ZooKeeper possesses:

- ZooKeeper, being a coordination service, also acts as a distributed application on its own.

- ZooKeeper follows a client-server architecture where clients are the nodes that avail the service and servers are the service providers.

- You might have heard about the ZooKeeper ensemble, which is just a group of ZooKeeper servers.

- In a specific timestamp, one ZooKeeper client can connect to only one ZooKeeper server.

- In a specific timestamp, a single ZooKeeper server is capable enough to tackle a huge number of clients connecting to it.

- Each ZooKeeper client pings the ZooKeeper server intermittently to ensure that it is alive and running healthily. In return, the server acknowledges the client's ping to communicate that it is still alive and healthy. In case the client doesn't receive the acknowledgments from the server within a specific time frame, it assumes that the server has gone for a toss and it silently connects to another server from the server pool (ensemble). Thus, the client session is quietly switched over to a new ZooKeeper server.

Now, let us have a glance at the following diagram that depicts the client-server architecture that ZooKeeper possesses:

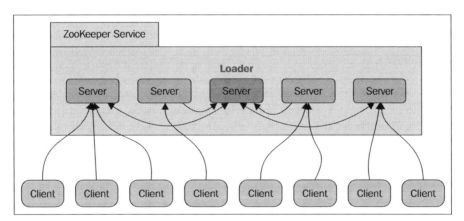

ZooKeeper has a filesystem-based data model that constitutes of **ZooKeeper data nodes (znodes)**. We can consider znodes as files in a Unix-based system, with the difference being that they can have child nodes. To understand this better, let us look at the following diagram that represents the hierarchy of software organizations operational in two cities.

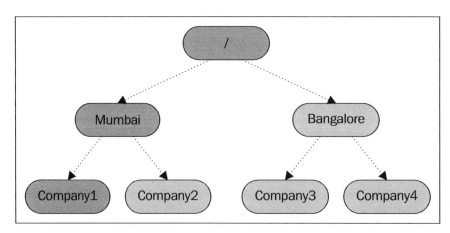

Each of the ZooKeeper servers stores the znode hierarchy within its memory, which enables the server to scale and respond to the client's read requests promptly. All write requests to each ZooKeeper server is logged in a transaction log that resides on the disk and is maintained by the respective server. This transaction log also plays a vital role in terms of performance, due to the fact that it is mandatory for the ZooKeeper server to synchronize transactions to the disk before it returns the success response. The maximum size of data that is permitted to be stored in a znode is 1 MB. Thus, it should only be used to store a small amount of data that is necessary to facilitate availability, reliability, and coordination to the distributed application.

When a client requests for a znode, the read operation takes place on the server that the client is connected to. Since only one server from the pool of servers is connected to a client, the read operations are quite fast. On the contrary, quite a number of servers from the ensembles are required to commence a write operation successfully. One of the nodes from the ensemble is elected as the leader. When a write request comes up to a server, this server passes the request to the leader to take appropriate action. The leader then broadcasts the request to all the servers available in the ensemble. If a strict majority of the nodes (also termed as the **quorum**) respond successfully to this write request, only then will the request be considered as successful, and the returned code is triggered back to the client who initiated this request.

Setting an ideal node count for ZooKeeper

Let us now understand a few facts about ZooKeeper in an intention to know what the ideal node count (server count) is that one should implement and why. You may have only one node in the ensemble; however, it wouldn't be considered a reliable and available system. If you have two nodes in the ensemble, you should have both the nodes always up and running due to the fact that one of the two nodes can't be considered as a quorum. Assume that you have three nodes in your ensemble and one of them went for a toss. Despite this, we still have two nodes that are quorum and they will keep the services up and running. This is why the ZooKeeper ensemble constitutes of an odd number of nodes. Moreover, having four nodes doesn't provide you extra benefit in terms of fault tolerance as compared to that of having three.

To figure out how to decide the node count, let us keep a few things in mind. Firstly, in the case of the read operation, the node count doesn't matter due to the fact that the client and server have a one-on-one connection, and its performance doesn't have any impact based on the total number of nodes available in the ensemble. Secondly, when it comes to the write operation, it can only be successful when it is written to the quorum of nodes. The write operation's performance is inversely proportional to the number of nodes in the ensemble. This also means that when you increase the node count in your ensemble, the write performance will degrade because the write operation would require more servers to interact with each other to serve the request.

Setting up, configuring, and deploying ZooKeeper

By now, we know what ZooKeeper is, its architecture, and how it works. It's time to learn how to set up, configure, and deploy our ZooKeeper ensemble, and we will learn how to do it in this section.

For demonstration purposes, we will use ZooKeeper Version 3.4.5, which is the latest version of ZooKeeper at the time of writing. Moreover, we have considered using three ZooKeeper nodes with the names `znode1.smohan.dom`, `znode2.smohan.dom`, and `znode3.smohan.dom`. So let us get started by following the proceeding steps on each node.

Setting up ZooKeeper

If you don't have JDK installed, download and install it. We recommend that you refer to *Chapter 1, Installing Solr*, to learn how to install it. Additionally, JDK is required as the ZooKeeper server runs on JVM. We can set up ZooKeeper by performing the following steps:

1. Download `zooKeeper-3.4.5.tar.gz` and untar it to an appropriate location using the following command:

    ```
    wget http://supergsego.com/apache/zookeeper/stable/
    zookeeper3.4.5.tar.gz tar xzvf zookeeper3.4.5.tar.gz
    ```

2. We create a directory as a root so as to store state associated to the ZooKeeper server. To do so, we run the following command:

    ```
    mkdir /var/lib/zookeeper
    ```

Configuring ZooKeeper

Now, we will configure ZooKeeper. To do so, perform the following steps:

1. Navigate to `zookeeper3.4.5/conf/` and create or edit (whichever is applicable) the file with the name `zoo.cfg`, and populate it with the following information:

    ```
    tickTime=1800
    dataDir=/var/lib/zookeeper
    clientPort=2080
    initLimit=5
    syncLimit=2
    server.1=znode1.smohan.dom:2999:3999
    server.2=znode2.smohan.dom:2999:3999
    server.3=znode3.smohan.dom:2999:3999
    ```

    The explanation of the preceding information is as follows:

    o   `port 2080`: This is used as the ZooKeeper client

    o   `port 2999`: This is used by peer ZooKeeper servers to communicate among themselves

    o   `port 3999`: This is used for leader election

    We need to make sure that all the preceding ports are open on all the machines to ensure uninterrupted communication.

2. We now create a ZID file and place it in the `/var/lib/zookeeper` directory. The contents of this file will vary based on the server it resides on. For instance, the ZID file at `znode1.smohan.dom` would contain 1 (a numerical number), `znode2.smohan.dom` will contain 2, and so on. For demo purposes, let us run the following `cat` command on this ZID file while we are in `znode2.smohan.dom`:

```
surendra@znode2.smohan.dom:~# cat /var/lib/zookeeper/zid
```

The output of the preceding command is as follows:

```
2
```

Deploying ZooKeeper

Now, it's time to start the ZooKeeper servers on each of the machines. To do so, we need to perform the following steps:

1. We need to run the following script:

```
zookeeper3.4.5/bin/zkServer.sh start
```

2. We are now ready to start a CLI client from one of our machines that run the ZooKeeper server. Here, we want the client to supply the list of servers so that in case one of them goes for a toss, the other server from this list is chosen and the client's session gets transferred to that server. To do so, we run the following script:

```
Zookeeper3.4.5/bin/zkCli.sh server znode1.smohan.dom:2080, znode2.smohan.dom:2080, znode3.smohan.dom:2080
```

3. Once the client has started, we can now create, edit, and delete znodes. Let us start with creating a znode `/firstnode` with some dummy data (for instance, `FirstNodeContent`) associated with it. To do so, we run the `create` command as follows along with its output:

```
[zk: 127.0.0.1:2080(CONNECTED) 3] create /firstnode

FirstNodeContent

Created /firstnode
```

4. As you can see, our znode has been created. It's now time to verify and retrieve the data associated with this znode. To do so, we run the `get` command, as shown in the following screenshot along with its output:

```
[zk: 127.0.0.1:2080(CONNECTED) 5] get /firstnode
FirstNodeContent
cZxid = 0x200000003
ctime = Fri Jan 17 15:51:36 IST 2014
mZxid = 0x200000003
mtime = Fri Jan 17 15:51:36 IST 2014
pZxid = 0x200000003
cversion = 0
dataVersion = 0
aclVersion = 0
ephemeralOwner = 0x0
dataLength = 16
numChildren = 0
```

In the preceding output, you must have noticed that along with the data associated with the znode, the client also returned some associated metadata. The `ctime` and `mtime` parameters denote the created and last modified timestamps of the znode respectively. The `dataVersion` parameter denotes the version of the data and it changes every time the data is modified. The `dataLength` parameter states the length of the data and `numChildren` denotes the number of children this znode has.

5. Now, let us remove our znode `/firstnode`. To do so, we run the following command:

```
[zk: 127.0.0.1:2080(CONNECTED) 2] rmr /firstnode
```

6. Since we have already deleted the `znode`, let us create another one and learn how to use a different parameter. To do so, we will create another znode `/secondnode` with the `SecondNodeContent` content and explore further. To do so, we will run the `create` command as follows (the command with its output is shown):

```
[zk: 127.0.0.1:2080(CONNECTED) 9] create /secondnode
SecondNodeContent
Created /secondnode
```

7. Now, let us verify and fetch the data at /secondnode. However, this time, the difference would be that we will be appending an optional parameter 1 at the end of the command. This parameter sets a one-time trigger (also known as watch) for the content at /secondnode. In case some other client modifies the content at /secondnode, a one-time notification will be sent to the first client for the modification made by the other client. Since it is a one-time notification, you will receive it only for the first instance of the modification, and later, it will be ignored. If you want the notification to be triggered again, the watch needs to be set again. The following screenshot shows the get command that we run along with the output that sets the watch:

```
[zk: 127.0.0.1:2080(CONNECTED) 13] get /secondnode
1
SecondNodeContent
cZxid = 0x200000005
ctime = Fri Jan 17 15:55:21 IST 2014
mZxid = 0x200000005
mtime = Fri Jan 17 15:55:21 IST 2014
pZxid = 0x200000005
cversion = 0
dataVersion = 0
aclVersion = 0
ephemeralOwner = 0x0
dataLength = 17
numChildren = 0
```

8. Now, we will change the data associated to /secondnode from some other client. The following screenshot shows the command and the output chunk demonstrating this:

```
[zk: 127.0.0.2:2080(CONNECTED) 2] set /secondnode
SecondNodeContentRevision1
cZxid = 0x200000005
ctime = Fri Jan 17 15:55:21 IST 2014
mZxid = 0x200000008
mtime = Fri Jan 17 16:20:35 IST 2014
pZxid = 0x200000005
cversion = 0
dataVersion = 1
aclVersion = 0
ephemeralOwner = 0x0
dataLength = 26
numChildren = 0
```

9. On execution of the preceding command, we received the following watch notification on the first client:

```
[zk: 127.0.0.1:2080(CONNECTED) 11]

WATCHER::

WatchedEvent state:SyncConnected type:NodeDataChanged path:/
secondnode
```

10. Since znodes form a hierarchical structure, we may also create their children, that is, subnodes. Let us now create a child node as follows:

```
[zk: 127.0.0.1:2080(CONNECTED) 1] create /secondnode/

subnode 123

Created /secondnode/

Subnode
```

11. Finally, let us learn how to fetch additional stat-related metadata about any znode. We fetch it by running the stat command as follows:

```
[zk: 127.0.0.1:2080(CONNECTED) 6] stat /secondnode
cZxid = 0x200000005
ctime = Fri Jan 17 15:55:21 IST 2014
mZxid = 0x200000008
mtime = Fri Jan 17 16:20:35 IST 2014
pZxid = 0x20000001
acversion = 1
dataVersion = 1
aclVersion = 0
ephemeralOwner = 0x0
dataLength = 26
numChildren = 1
```

Applications of ZooKeeper

Due to its versatile role in a distributed system, ZooKeeper has a huge set of practical applications already in the market. We will list a few of them here in this section as follows:

- **Apache Solr**: It uses ZooKeeper to elect the leader (that is, the leader election process) and centralize the configuration

- **Apache Hadoop**: It seeks the help of ZooKeeper to automatically recover from Hadoop HDFS Namenode failure, thereby providing high availability of YARN ResourceManager

- **Apache Accumulo**: It is a sorted distributed key-value store that is built on top of Apache ZooKeeper and Apache Hadoop

- **Apache HBase**: It is a distributed database that is built on Hadoop, ZooKeeper facilitates it with master election, lease management, and communication among servers

- **Apache Mesos**: It is used to manage clusters and provides effective resource sharing and isolation across distributed applications. ZooKeeper helps Mesos in facilitating a replicating master that is fault tolerant

- **Cloudera Search**: It uses ZooKeeper for centralized configuration management purposes and is used to integrate search features with Apache Hadoop

- **Neo4j**: It is a graph database for distributed systems and uses ZooKeeper to write master selection and read slave coordination

Summary

In this chapter, we learned how to use ZooKeeper for performance optimization purposes, and we covered how to set up, configure, and deploy ZooKeeper. We also learned about the different applications of ZooKeeper that can help us optimize Solr's performance.

In the next chapter, we will list down some useful and necessary references to the official and documentation pages that will help you to explore the topics and concepts even further. It also covers the recommended books and video tutorials that will facilitate you to enhance your learning curve.

Resources

The following list consists of important resource links that will help you explore further and understand the topics covered in the preceding chapters better:

- XAMPP for Windows at `http://www.apachefriends.org/en/xampp-windows.html`, with reference to *Chapter 1*, *Installing Solr*. You may visit this link if you want to download the latest XAMPP installer for Windows.

- The Tomcat add-on at `http://tomcat.apache.org/download-60.cgi`, as discussed in *Chapter 1*, *Installing Solr*. In order to run Apache Solr, you need an application server (Tomcat, Jetty, and so on). This link will help you find and download the necessary add-on for Tomcat.

- Java JDK at `http://java.sun.com/javase/downloads/index.jsp`, with reference to *Chapter 1*, *Installing Solr*. Since Apache Solr is Java based, it requires Java JDK to function appropriately. This link will help you find and download the latest version of Java JDK.

- Apache Solr at `http://lucene.apache.org/solr/`, as discussed in *Chapter 1*, *Installing Solr*. You need to set up Apache Solr on your machine to avail its benefits. This link will help you with the latest version of Apache Solr. Additionally, it provides you with a documentation to understand more about Solr.

- The Solr PHP client at `http://code.google.com/p/solr-php-client/`, with reference to *Chapter 1*, *Installing Solr*. This link helps you with the client-side code and is used only when you wish to implement Solr for a PHP-based application.

- The Solr Wiki page at `http://en.wikipedia.org/wiki/Apache_Solr`. To know more about Apache Solr, you may also visit this link, which is its Wiki page.

- The similarity class at `http://lucene.apache.org/core/4_0_0/core/org/apache/lucene/search/similarities/Similarity.html`, as discussed in *Chapter 2, Boost Your Search*. If you are eager to explore further the parameters affecting the scores, this link is for you.

- The `SweetSpotSimilarity` class at `http://lucene.apache.org/core/3_0_3/api/contrib-misc/org/apache/lucene/misc/SweetSpotSimilarity.html`, with reference to *Chapter 2, Boost Your Search*. In case none of the setups work out for you while troubleshooting your queries and scoring, you may try out using the `SweetSpotSimilarity` class and this link will help you learn even further.

- The Haversine formula at `http://bigdatanerd.wordpress.com/2011/11/03/java-implementation-of-haversine-formula-for-distance-calculation-between-two-points/`, as discussed in *Chapter 2, Boost Your Search*. You may need to use the Haversine formula in order to calculate distance between two geographical points. You may refer this link to explore it further.

- The HTTP cache header at `http://www.w3.org/Protocols/rfc2616/rfc2616-sec13.html`, with reference to *Chapter 3, Performance Optimization*. You need to understand the HTTP cache header before you learn how to cache the result pages. This link contains the HTTP Cache Header RFC document, which will help you keep pace with the topics covered in the chapter.

- Apache's ZooKeeper installer at `http://supergsego.com/apache/zookeeper/stable/`, as discussed in *Chapter 6, Performance Optimization with ZooKeeper*. This link will help you find the appropriate stable version of the ZooKeeper installer for your machine.

- Apache ZooKeeper documentation at `http://zookeeper.apache.org/`, with reference to *Chapter 6, Performance Optimization with ZooKeeper*. This link will help you with the documentation of ZooKeeper.

- Apache Hadoop at `http://hadoop.apache.org/`, as discussed in *Chapter 6, Performance Optimization with ZooKeeper*. With the help of this link, you should be able to know more about Apache Hadoop.

- Apache Accumulo at `http://accumulo.apache.org/`, with reference to *Chapter 6, Performance Optimization with ZooKeeper*. You may learn about Apache Accumulo by navigating to this link.

- Apache HBase at `http://hbase.apache.org/`, as discussed in *Chapter 6, Performance Optimization with ZooKeeper*. This link will guide you to understand Apache HBase in depth.

- Apache Mesos at `http://mesos.apache.org/`, with reference to *Chapter 6, Performance Optimization with ZooKeeper*. You may find the official documentation of Apache Mesos in this link.

- Cloudera search at `https://github.com/cloudera/search`, as referenced in *Chapter 6, Performance Optimization with ZooKeeper*. You may visit this link to learn about Cloudera Search and get the code base to practice.

- Neo4j at `http://www.neo4j.org/`, with respect to *Chapter 6, Performance Optimization with ZooKeeper*. This link will provide you the documentation to learn about Neo4j.

The following is the list of a few books and video tutorials from Packt Publishing, which might interest you and help you understand Apache Solr and its features better:

- *Administrating Solr* found at `http://www.packtpub.com/administrate-monitor-and-optimize-solr-using-drupal-associated-scripts/book`

- *Apache Solr 3.1 Cookbook* found at `http://www.packtpub.com/solr-3-1-enterprise-search-server-cookbook/book`

- *Apache Solr 4 Cookbook* found at `http://www.packtpub.com/apache-solr-4-cookbook/book`

- *Apache Solr 3 Enterprise Search Server* found at `http://www.packtpub.com/apache-solr-3-enterprise-search-server/book`

- *Getting Started with Apache Solr Search Server* found at `http://www.packtpub.com/content/getting-started-apache-solr-search-server/video`

Index

H

Hadoop. *See* Apache Hadoop
Haversine formula
  URL 31, 102
HBase. *See* Apache HBase
homophones
  searching for 67, 68
HTTP cache header
  URL 102

I

ideal node count
  setting, for ZooKeeper 93
implementation, near real-time search
    (NRT)
  challenges 58, 59
index size
  truncating 77-79
index-time 15
index-time boosting 15, 16
infinite loop exception
  dealing with, in shards 82, 83
installation, Apache Solr
  prerequisites 7, 8
installation, Apache Solr components 8-12
inverse document frequency (idf) 14
inverse reciprocal, function query 34, 35

J

Java JDK
  URL 101
  URL, for downloading 7

L

linear, function query 34
locked index
  dealing with 77
logarithm, function query 32, 33
Lucene DisjunctionMaxQuery
  about 19
  versus, dismax query parser 19, 20
lucene query parser 26
Lucene query parser
  versus, dismax query parser 18, 19

M

mathematical operations, function query
    28, 29
memory usage 38
Mesos. *See* Apache Mesos
ms() function 30
mul() function 24
multiple opened files
  dealing with 79, 80

N

near real-time search (NRT)
  about 58
  implementing 58, 59
  versus, real-time search 58
Neo4j
  about 99
  URL 103

O

optimize command 76
ord() function 29
out-of-memory
  dealing with 81
  Wiki reference 81

P

partial phrase boosting 22
performance optimization, Apache Solr 61
predefined words
  filtering out, from being searched 69-71

Q

query
  troubleshooting 16-18
query (q, def?) function 30
query result caching 39, 40
query-time
  about 15
  boosting 15, 16
quorum 92

Thank you for buying
Apache Solr High Performance

About Packt Publishing

Packt, pronounced 'packed', published its first book "*Mastering phpMyAdmin for Effective MySQL Management*" in April 2004 and subsequently continued to specialize in publishing highly focused books on specific technologies and solutions.

Our books and publications share the experiences of your fellow IT professionals in adapting and customizing today's systems, applications, and frameworks. Our solution based books give you the knowledge and power to customize the software and technologies you're using to get the job done. Packt books are more specific and less general than the IT books you have seen in the past. Our unique business model allows us to bring you more focused information, giving you more of what you need to know, and less of what you don't.

Packt is a modern, yet unique publishing company, which focuses on producing quality, cutting-edge books for communities of developers, administrators, and newbies alike. For more information, please visit our website: www.packtpub.com.

About Packt Open Source

In 2010, Packt launched two new brands, Packt Open Source and Packt Enterprise, in order to continue its focus on specialization. This book is part of the Packt Open Source brand, home to books published on software built around Open Source licences, and offering information to anybody from advanced developers to budding web designers. The Open Source brand also runs Packt's Open Source Royalty Scheme, by which Packt gives a royalty to each Open Source project about whose software a book is sold.

Writing for Packt

We welcome all inquiries from people who are interested in authoring. Book proposals should be sent to author@packtpub.com. If your book idea is still at an early stage and you would like to discuss it first before writing a formal book proposal, contact us; one of our commissioning editors will get in touch with you.

We're not just looking for published authors; if you have strong technical skills but no writing experience, our experienced editors can help you develop a writing career, or simply get some additional reward for your expertise.

Instant Apache Wicket 6

ISBN: 978-1-78328-001-8 eBook: 54 pages

Learn how to get started with Apache Wicket 6

1. Learn something new in an Instant! A short, fast, focused guide delivering immediate results.

2. Learn to build a Wicket application.

3. Get to grips with the core concepts of Wicket.

4. Understand the lifecycle of Wicket.

Apache Solr Beginner's Guide

ISBN: 978-1-78216-252-0 Paperback: 324 pages

Configure your own search engine experience with real-world data with this practical guide to Apache Solr

1. Learn to use Solr in real-world contexts, even if you are not a programmer, using simple configuration examples.

2. Define simple configurations for searching data in several ways in your specific context, from suggestions to advanced faceted navigation.

3. Teaches you in an easy-to-follow style, full of examples, illustrations, and tips to suit the demands of beginners.

Please check **www.PacktPub.com** for information on our titles

34856601R00071

Made in the USA
Lexington, KY
21 August 2014